P9-CTB-613

RELEASED

Free Transit

Charles River Associates Incorporated is a professional service organization in Cambridge, Massachusetts, that specializes in economic and econometric research. CRA has conducted research in the fields of transportation, pollution control and abatement, and natural resource industries, among others. CRA's work is generally performed for long-range planning and policy formulating groups in industry and government.

Free Transit

A Charles River Associates Research Study

HE4461.D65 ST. JOSEPH'S UNIVERSITY STX
Free transit

3 9353 00088 9624

HE
4461
D65

Thomas A. Domencich
Gerald Kraft

Charles River Associates
Incorporated

Heath Lexington Books
D. C. Heath and Company
Lexington, Massachusetts

129370

Copyright © 1970 by D. C. Heath and Company

All rights reserved. No part of this publication may be reproduced or transmitted in any form or by any means, electronic or mechanical, including photocopy, recording, or any information storage or retrieval system, without permission in writing from the publisher.

Portions of this book have previously appeared as part of *An Evaluation of Free Transit Service* prepared for the Department of Transportation by Charles River Associates Incorporated. No claim of copyright is entered for any part of this book taken verbatim from the prior report.

Printed in the United States of America

Library of Congress Number: 79-116833

Table of Contents

Tables and Figures

Authors' Preface

We wish to acknowledge the support of the U. S. Department of Transportation, as this volume is based on a research study prepared for them: *An Evaluation of Free Transit Service,* Charles River Associates Incorporated, prepared for the Office of Economics, Assistant Secretary for Policy Development, Department of Transportation, Washington, D. C., Contract Number T8-088 (Neg.), Report Number 125-1. Special thanks are due to James C. Nelson, then Director of the Office of Economics (DOT), and Walter Velona, the project monitor, for their generous help and interest in the study.

We also wish to thank Mahlon Straszheim and Paul Roberts of Harvard University, Alex Friedlander of the New York City Transit Authority, and David McNicol and Carol MacMurray of Charles River Associates, for their extensive contributions to the original research. Finally, we thank the many officials of the Massachusetts Bay Transportation Authority who generously provided data and other valuable assistance. The views expressed in this paper are solely those of the authors, and do not necessarily reflect the official policy of the Department of Transportation or the Massachusetts Bay Transportation Authority.

Free Transit

1

Purpose and Scope of the Study

The provision of transportation services is a continuing responsibility for all metropolitan centers, and in very many cities it is far too immediate and deep a problem to be regarded in any sense as routine.

Urban transportation planning is much more difficult than interurban planning. Although many benefits can be attributed to new urban highways, the land-takings required for highway construction may break up established neighborhoods, giving rise to serious social disruption. Highways may run through parks or violate waterfront views, thereby impairing the aesthetic quality of the city. They may reduce the urban tax base, thereby making the solution of many other public problems more difficult. To be sure there have been many difficulties in constructing the intercity portion of the interstate highway system, but they were small in comparison to the problems that are being encountered by highway planners in urban areas. It is planned that during the coming decade the urban portion of the interstate highway system will be completed. It is now commonly agreed that these urban highways, representing about 15 percent of the mileage in the interstate system, will account for about half of the cost of the system and probably 90 percent of the problems.

Nevertheless, there is growing agitation in the cities over rush-hour traffic congestion. There is no compelling factual evidence that rush-hour congestion is growing worse over time. Indeed the fragmentary evidence suggests that, in spite of almost a doubling of the number of cars in use, the performance of the urban highway system is considerably better now than it was in the immediate postwar years. In most cities sizeable increases in highway capacity, coupled with little or no increase in travel demands in the core city as a result of job and residence dispersion, have actually caused auto trip times to decline slightly in the postwar period. Dissatisfaction with urban highway performance seems to be more the result of rising expectations than decreasing performance, although demands for improved highway performance are no less real or urgent for being based on increased expectations. Confronted with increased demands for highway improvements, yet faced with growing hostility from those who believe the urban freeways are disrupting and deteriorating the urban environment, highway planners have felt a mounting sense of frustration and futility.

In many cities there have been calls for a new emphasis on public transit planning. Increasingly, massive investments in rapid transit facilities are being proposed as a solution to urban transportation problems. There have been recommendations for improvements in the collection and distribution system, such as more frequent scheduling and increased geographic coverage of the system, particularly new routes to serve cross-town trips. Such public transit services as express buses, downtown mini-bus services, increased use of jitneys, and various dual-mode vehicles are being proposed. It is argued that improved transit service will divert travelers from auto to public transit, thereby reducing highway congestion, parking problems, and air pollution, as well as decreasing the need for new highway construction so that land-takings and their attendant disruptions can be reduced.

Urban transportation planners are also being asked to contribute to a number of larger social objectives. In many communities the socially and economically disadvantaged are isolated from the rest of the community in ghettos, often located in areas relatively inaccessible to job opportunities. Transportation planners are being called on to provide ghetto residents with accessibility to job centers. People are looking to changes in the transportation system to rejuvenate the downtowns where retail sales have deteriorated as population, employment, and business activity have moved from the central city to the suburbs.

It is in this context that proposals have been made to provide free public transit service in our metropolitan areas. While much of the new emphasis in transportation planning has been concerned with the possible service improvements that could be developed to attract riders away from autos, there has also been growing interest in the reduction of fares as an incentive to use. This naturally leads to the consideration of a program of free transit, because this is probably the most dramatic fare incentive available and also because it provides the opportunity to eliminate the costs and inconveniences of fare collection.

The purpose of this study is to conduct an economic analysis of free transit service. The empirical findings are based largely on a case study of Boston. The principal conclusion of the study is that although free transit does, in general, contribute to the goals that its supporters seek to achieve, improved transit service is generally a more efficient means of promoting these objectives. The evidence indicates that transit ridership is more responsive to improvements in service than to reductions in fares. Reductions in access times to and from the transit station, as well as reductions in transfer and waiting times, are likely to be particularly important in this regard. The available evidence suggests, however, that even substantial improvements in transit services are not likely to reduce greatly the demand for automobile travel.

The main body of the study begins with Chapter 2. This chapter discusses the responsiveness of urban passenger travelers to changes in travel time and cost. Both auto and transit trip behavior are examined by means of an econometric model of urban passenger demand developed from Boston data. Chapter 3 describes the effects of free transit service on the performance of the transit and highway system and discusses changes in technology and operating policies which are available to increase transit's share of the urban passenger market. In chapter 4 we examine the effects of free transit on Boston's transit ridership and the associated costs. Using the results of Chapters 2 and 3, estimates are made of the increased ridership resulting from the free fare, the costs of accommodating the extra riders, and the likely savings from eliminating the expenses associated with fare collection.

Chapter 5 presents the gross estimates of cost for nationwide free transit service. These figures are based on estimates of the nationwide cost of operating the present transit service, plus the increase in service that is indicated by the Boston figures developed in Chapter 4.

In Chapter 6 we evaluate the effectiveness of free transit in meeting various objectives and compare it to service improvements or other alternative means of achieving the same goals. Chapter 7 describes the administrative considerations which would result from implementing a program of free transit service and discusses the income redistributional considerations which should be evaluated in analyzing a program of free transit. Recommendations for future research are presented in Chapter 8. Finally, the principal conclusions of the study are summarized in Chapter 9.

2

The Demand for Urban Passenger Travel

Introduction

In order to identify and evaluate the effects of any transit subsidy program, urban passenger travel behavior must be understood. The effects of a reduction in transit fares on transit ridership and on auto traffic must be determined. In addition, the effects of changes in the various aspects of transit service on both transit and auto travel, must be understood in order to be able to evaluate fare subsidies in comparison with transit service subsidies. This is the subject of the present chapter.

It is generally possible to find from published data how many riders a given city's transit system has carried during each of several recent years. In any particular year, however, these trips were the product of existing conditions. As any program of public subsidy contemplates changing the terms upon which transit service is offered, there is little reason to suppose that raw historical data are a useful indication of what ridership would be upon implementation of a new policy program. The relevant knowledge about the behavior of ridership should, rather, be summarized in a statistical demand function which relates ridership to system performance variables. Then as the performance of the system is changed by the implementation of a policy program, the resulting effect on travel demand can be estimated.

Estimating the demand for transit also clearly requires consideration of automobile travel. It is reasonable to think of transit and auto trips as differentiated but competing products, in a single transportation market. From this point of view, the characteristics of each mode influence the demand for the other. The cost and travel time of automobile travel influence the demand for transit and, conversely, transit fares, frequency, and travel time influence the number of automobile trips. Two related statistical demand models, therefore, are required, one for transit and one for automobile.

In view of the widespread interest and the considerable sums of money that have been spent on urban transportation planning, one might expect a substantial number of satisfactory models to be available. Unfortunately, this is not the case. A large number of urban demand forecasting studies have been made, but surprisingly little is known about the behavioral dimensions of urban passenger travel. Almost no one has made an attempt to model the decision-making process that the traveler goes through and as a result, knowledge of the causal relationships, which is needed to evaluate policy alternatives, is very scanty. Most of the modeling which has been done has concentrated on searching for statistical regularities in the historical data without much regard for the causal implications of the model.

In this chapter of the report we will present a fairly detailed description of a model of urban travel demand which was developed recently by Charles River Associates (CRA) and seeks to correct these deficiencies. This model is used extensively in later chapters of the report so a lengthy discussion of its development is warranted. This model is a substantial improvement over the "gravity" models that have been developed in most urban transportation studies, but there are still significant shortcomings and our knowledge of urban travel behavior remains far more primitive than it ought to be.

These shortcomings will be discussed in the presentation which follows, but it may be useful to describe beforehand the most important limitation of the model, namely that it does not take account of the interrelationships between the transportation system and urban development. The effect of urban development on passenger travel demand is modeled, but the feedback – the effect of transportation facilities on urban development – is not incorporated. Thus, the long-run impact of changes in the transportation system on the location of jobs, residences, shopping facilities, etc., and the consequent effect of these decisions on trip-making, is not taken into account. Instead the land-use pattern is taken as a given, determined independently of the transportation system. This practice has been followed in almost all urban transportation studies and therefore our knowledge of the long-run impact of changes in the transportation system on travel demand is almost wholly lacking. The few studies which have attempted to model the interrelationship between land-use and the transportation system have, in our opinion, not been very well conceived and their results are not very useful.

Modeling Urban Passenger Travel Behavior[a]

In developing a model of urban travel demand, it is useful to approach the

[a]This discussion draws heavily on the following publications: *A Model of Urban Passenger Travel Demand in the San Francisco Metropolitan Area,* Charles River Associates Incorporated (prepared for Peat, Marwick, Livingston & Co. in conjunction with their study for the California Division of Bay Toll Crossings) December 1967; Gerald Kraft and Martin Wohl, "New Directions for Passenger Demand Analysis and Forecasting," *Transportation Research,* Vol. 1, No. 3, Pergamon Press, 1967; and, T.A. Domencich, G. Kraft and J.P. Valette, "Estimation of Urban Passenger Travel Behavior: An Economic Demand Model," *Highway Research Record,* Number 238, (1968) Highway Research Board, National Academy of Science – National Academy of Engineering.

The genesis of CRA's work on urban travel demand was an earlier study of intercity travel demand directed by G. Kraft, Part V of *Demand for Intercity Passenger Travel in the Washington-Boston Corridor,* Systems Analysis and Research Corporation, Boston, Massachusetts.

problem by considering the individual. Although we are concerned with aggregates of people, their behavior can probably best be understood by considering the behavior of individual travelers. We would like to know what decisions the traveler faces in his travel behavior, and what factors influence these decisions.

The individual traveler has a set of choices to make. He must decide whether to make a trip at all, where to go, which route to take, which mode to use, and when to go.[b] Each of these choices has an associated set of values and costs (in money and time) for the individual; the values themselves will vary with the trip's purpose and sometimes with the time of day, On a moment's reflection, it is clear that these choices are not independent. The costs of the various modes influence not only the choice of mode but also the selection of destination and the determination of whether the trip should be made at all. For example, an improvement in the freeway system which reduces the travel time to the downtown area may not only divert shoppers from secondary shopping centers to downtown and shift travelers from transit to auto, it may also stimulate an increase in the total number of shopping trips. Mounting congestion, on the other hand, may reduce the total number of shopping trips by making each trip more effective and well planned.

Similarly, the attractiveness of a destination may influence both the distribution of trips between destinations and the number of trips that are made. Rejuvenating the downtown area, for example, or building a new stadium or concert hall, may not only redistribute shopping, social, and recreational trips between zones; it may also draw housewives or families out of the home and thereby increase the total number of trips made.

The alternatives available to individuals determine not only their selection of modes and destination zones, but also the total number of trips that they make. If conditions are favorable, the individual may make many trips; if all the available alternatives are poor, he may make few trips or even no trips at all. Because the value of the trip depends on its ultimate objective, we might expect shopping, personal business, social, and recreational trips to be more sensitive to these conditions than work trips. However, nonwork trips comprise a large and growing percentage of all trips, constituting in most cities the majority or close to the majority of trips. In the Boston metropolitan area, for example, they comprise 63 percent of all trips. This makes it essential that the responsiveness of passenger travel demand to time and cost conditions be incorporated into a model of travel behavior.

The approach usually taken in the analysis of urban travel demand separates the problem into elements of trip generation, attraction, distribution, assignment to routes, and modal split. As the above discussion indicates, however, these choices are so intertwined that they are best treated as being made simultaneously rather than separately.

The separate treatment of these elements in the currently popular models has several related consequences. First, it results in the implicit assumption that the number of trips generated is independent of the performance of the transpor-

[b]In addition, of course, he has a locational decision. He must decide where to live. As discussed above, the CRA demand model assumes that the locational decision has been settled and only models the travel decisions.

tation system. That is, it is assumed that changes in travel time or cost can influence the modal split or distribution of trips between zonal pairs, but cannot change the total number of trips generated. By assumption, the models assert that the policies implemented by transportation planners have no effect on the total number of trips made! It is possible that changes in the transportation system will not affect trip generation, but there is no good reason for making this assumption *a priori*. It seems better to avoid it altogether and to let the question be settled through the results of empirical estimation.

Second, the separation of these elements probably leads to improper measurement of the effect of the independent variables in the individual trip generation and attraction equations. To clarify this, consider a comparison between a family living a substantial distance from the nearest shopping area and a family living relatively near a shopping center. Assume that the first family is large, is relatively wealthy, and has several autos, while the second family is moderate in size, is relatively poor, and has one automobile. Other things the same, we would expect more shopping trips from the larger family with the higher income and greater number of autos. If the effect of car ownership or family size on trip generation were measured from these two observations, however, the opposite would appear to be true because the time, cost, and related inconvenience of travel have been left out of the comparison, and their effects on travel behavior have been attributed to socioeconomic variables. As the example illustrates, improperly specifying the trip generation and attraction equations by omitting relevant variables may cause the effects of the variables actually included in the equations to be confounded with the effects of the omitted variables and consequently cause them to be improperly measured.[c]

A further shortcoming of most extant demand models concerns the calibration procedure used in distributing trips to zonal pairs. Several forms of trip distribution models are in use, the most common being the gravity model. In the gravity model the estimated number of trips between a given pair of zones depends on the estimated number of trips generated by the origin zone, the estimated number of trips attracted by the destination zone, and the "friction" between the two zones. In calibrating the trip distribution model the parameters of the friction factor are adjusted until a close reproduction of the frequency distribution of trip lengths is obtained. The practice of using the frequency distribution of trip lengths as a criterion of performance on which to calibrate the distribution model is an obvious error. The purpose of the model is to explain interzonal trips, not the frequency distribution of trip lengths and the model should be calibrated on the basis of its ability to reproduce zone-to-zone trips. If zone-to-zone travel is faithfully reproduced, the frequency distribution of trip lengths will also be reproduced, but the converse does not necessarily hold.

The next section describes how the different elements of choice can be represented in a single model which, to the extent that it can be made to represent the effects of each element of travel behavior, can provide answers to the significant policy questions posed. Furthermore, by incorporating the

[c]For a thorough discussion of specification errors, see Zvi Griliches, *The Analysis of Specification Errors* (mimeograph), Department of Economics, University of Chicago.

transportation system characteristics explicitly in the model, the planner can investigate the consequences of alternative policies on tripmaking behavior, facilitating the accomplishment of policy objectives.

Model Specification and Variables

The CRA model is based on conventional economic theory, the theory of consumer behavior. Economic theory provides us with useful guidelines for specifying a demand model: first, because it identifies in a broad, general way the variables that influence demand; and second, because it specifies the general nature of the relationship between these variables and demand. The variables identified by the theory of consumer behavior as relevant in a study of demand are the price of the good or service being investigated, the prices of competing or complementary goods or services, and income.

For urban auto passenger demand the subject commodity has at least two prices which must be considered, automobile travel time and cost. Travel time is considered part of the price of a trip because it is an important part of the disutility of travel. The prices of competing goods are the times and costs of travel by the available transit modes. For transit passenger demand, of course, the prices of the subject commodity are transit cost and travel time, while the relevant prices of substitutes are the times and costs of travel by auto. For auto, the prices of complementary goods are parking charges, toll fees, and the walking time to and from the car. For transit, they are the times and costs of access to and from the transit station.

Economic theory tells us that demand ordinarily will be negatively related to the prices of the subject commodity and positively related to the prices of substitutes. Demand will be negatively related to the prices of complements.

The relevant income variables include both the incomes of individuals (or households) in the urban area, and various measures of output of the activities which attract trips. Demand for most goods is usually positively related to the incomes of the individuals in the market for the good or service, although there are examples of goods for which the demand decreases as income goes up. People substitute a more desirable commondity for the good in question as their incomes rise.[d]

[d]Some people claim that the demand for transit decreases as income increases (*i.e.*, they claim it is an *inferior* good). Though not conclusive, our model lends some indirect support to this view, though not through the direct effects of the income variable. Transit demand in our model is sometimes positively, sometimes negatively related to income. However, it is generally negatively related to car ownership, which itself bears a strong positive relationship to income.

The need for measures of output of the activities which attract trips stems from transportation's role as a derived demand commodity. That is, transportation is usually not desired for its own sake but rather because it enables the traveler to satisfy another demand, *i.e.*, shopping, work, personal business, and so forth. Thus, some measure of the level of operations in the activity from which the demand for transportation is derived is needed in the transportation demand function. This requires disaggregating the trips by trip purpose and specifying relevant measures of activity for each trip purpose, *e.g.*, sales, employment, etc. These measures of activity are the usual attraction variables. All else equal, we expect the demand for transportation to be positively related to the level of operations of the activities served by transportation.

The above variables are appropriate for measuring individual demand behavior. Aggregate demand will, of course, be positively related to the number of individuals in the market and often will depend as well on various socioeconomic characteristics of these individuals, *e.g.*, age, occupation, family size, ethnic background, etc.

These ideas are incorporated in the following equation which is a general expression for the urban transportation demand model that we have developed:

$$N(i,j,i \mid Po,Mo,) = \phi[\underline{S}(i \mid Po), \underline{A}(j \mid Po), \underline{T}(i,j,i \mid Po,Mo),$$
$$\underline{C}(i,j,i \mid Po,Mo), \underline{T}(i,j,i \mid Po,M_\alpha),$$
$$\underline{C}(i,j,i \mid Po,M_\alpha)]$$

where

$N(i,j,i \mid Po,Mo)$	=	the number of round trips between origin i and destination j for purpose Po by mode Mo;
$\underline{S}(i \mid Po)$	=	a vector of socioeconomic characteristics appropriate to purpose Po describing the travelers residing in zone i;
$\underline{A}(j \mid Po)$	=	a vector of socioeconomic and land-use characteristics describing the level of activity appropriate to purpose Po in destination zone j;
$\underline{T}(i,j,i \mid Po,Mo)$	=	a vector of travel time components for the round trip from origin i to destination j for purpose Po by mode Mo;
$\underline{C}(i,j,i \mid Po,Mo)$	=	a vector of travel cost components for the round trip between origin i and destination j for purpose Po by mode Mo;

$\underline{T}(i,j,i\,|\,Po,M_\alpha)$ = a set of vectors of travel time components for the round trip between origin i and destination j, for purpose Po by each of the alternative modes ($\alpha = 1, \ldots, n$).

$\underline{\underline{C}}(i,j,i\,|\,Po,M_\alpha)$ = a set of vectors of travel cost components for the round trip between origin i and destination j for purpose Po by each of the alternative modes ($\alpha = 1, \ldots, n$).

In words, the equation says that the number of directed round trips between any zonal pair for a given purpose and mode is a function simultaneously of the number of individuals (or households) in the origin zone and their socio-economic characteristics, the appropriate measure of level of activity and other relevant socioeconomic and land-use characteristics in the destination zone, together with the round trip travel times and costs of the subject mode as well as those of competing modes. Times and costs of complementary services are included in the vectors of times and costs of the subject mode because they are also negatively related to demand and because it is often difficult in practice to distinguish the characteristics of the subject mode from those of its complementary services. There is an equation for each trip purpose and each mode.

Notice that the dependent variable is the interzonal round trip. This is because, first, this is the quantity of interest rather than the number of trips generated or attracted by a zone; and second, as discussed above, the simultaneity of the decisions about whether to make a trip at all, where to go, and which mode to use requires that the socioeconomic characteristics of the origin and destination zones be considered together, along with the trip times and costs required to travel between that specific zonal pair. This necessitates examination of zonal pair combinations.

It is preferable to analyze the round trip because time and cost conditions on both legs of the trip are considered by the traveler in making his trip decisions. Moreover, it is clear that selection of mode for the return trip usually depends on the modal choice made for the outbound trip, and the destination of the return trip usually depends on the origin of the outbound trip.

The choice of when to travel (*i.e.,* which hour of the day) is not reflected in the above model. This choice was omitted, not because it is unimportant, but rather because it substantially increases the size and complexity of the model and it was not possible to encompass this increased complexity within the time and budget limitations of the study for which this model was developed. This is an important shortcoming of the model because it means that no account has been taken of the diversions that take place between different hours of the day. For example, if rush-hour travel becomes increasingly more time-consuming relative to off-peak travel, some travelers will divert their trips to nonrush hours.

The model theoretically allows for consideration of a number of transit modes, but in its actual estimation all transit modes were aggregated into a single heterogeneous mode. This was not done by choice but rather because data were available only for the single heterogeneous mode within the time limitations of the study. This is particularly unfortunate for this study because the aggregation into a single mode of all transit modes — commuter rail, subway, bus, and streetcar — undoubtedly reduces the accuracy of the estimated relationships.

The independent variables in the model include the usual socioeconomic and land-use variables used in current models to measure trip generation and attraction as well as the system performance variables used to measure the time and costs to the traveler of making the trip by each of the alternative modes.

The socioeconomic and land-use variables tested in this study are straightforward and conventional, and need not be described in detail here.[e] They include population and population density (i.e., population per acre), personal income, car ownership, employment, and employment density for relevant industry groups, etc.

The system variables require lengthier comment because they are the relevant policy variables. First, because in the view of the user, all components of the trip probably contribute to its inconvenience, total door-to-door travel time and cost must be examined rather than only line-haul costs or times. Second, because travelers may react differently to different components of travel time and cost, it is desirable to disaggregate the times and costs into their component parts. Only in this way can answers to the policy questions required for this study be obtained.

The travel time by transit consists in a walk or drive to the station, the wait at the platform, the line-haul time, the time consumed in any transfers that have to be made, the walk from the terminating station to the final destination, and a component we choose to call schedule delay, which is any additional time that may be incurred because the arrival time allowed by the transit schedule may differ from the traveler's preferred arrival time. (If he has a 9:30 appointment, for example, and the nearest transit arrival time is 9:00, the traveler has a 30-minute schedule delay).

Similarly, the travel time by auto consists of the walk to the auto, the line-haul time, the parking time, the walk from the parking place to the destination, and the schedule delay. (If the auto traveler must leave early to get a parking place, for example, he suffers a schedule delay. Schedule delay for automobile travel also results from high congestion and queueing situations requiring tripmakers to arrive early in order to be on time for their appointments.)[f]

In other transportation demand studies there has been very little attempt made to disaggregate times and costs. Indeed in many of these studies only line-haul rather than door-to-door times and costs are considered. However, an examination of the transit proposals that are being widely discussed makes it clear that to be able to evaluate these proposals it is essential to be able to distinguish between the effects of reductions in line-haul time, out-of-vehicle time, and fares. Massive investments in rapid transit facilities continue to be proposed as a solution to urban transportation problems. At the same time, less

[e]A more complete discussion of these variables is available in Charles River Associates, op. cit.

[f]For a complete discussion of the concept of schedule delay see Kraft and Wohl, op. cit.

costly public transit services, such as express bus, downtown mini-bus services, increased use of jitneys, and various dual-mode vehicles, are also being proposed.

It is of considerable interest that some of these transit system proposals — rapid transit and express bus — emphasize improved line-haul speeds as a means of attracting riders from autos, while others — jitneys and mini-bus services — emphasize improved collection and distribution of passengers. The dual-mode vehicle, *i.e.*, a self-powered vehicle which can operate normally on city streets but can also be automatically controlled to become part of a high-speed train for arterial links of a trip, offers both improved door-to-door service and increased line-haul speeds. Jitneys, dual-mode vehicles and, to a slightly lesser extent, frequently scheduled mini-buses also compete with the freedom of departure and arrival times offered by the private automobile, whereas rapid transit and express and feeder bus services operate on fixed schedules and thus offer poor competition for this characteristic of private auto travel. An evaluation of these different transit modes requires an analysis of both the costs and benefits of the different services. There are substantial differences in the costs of the various services. Unless the higher costs of the more expensive services (*e.g.*, rapid transit) are compensated by a substantially greater stimulus to transit ridership, they should be deferred or rejected in favor of less costly improvements in transit services. However, to make this evaluation the planner needs a transportation demand model which expresses separately the effects of changes in line-haul times, collection and distribution times, and schedule delays. Without such a model it is difficult to see how these alternative transit proposals can be evaluated.

In our empirical research, travel time and cost were disaggregated into the following components: auto in-vehicle time, auto out-of-vehicle time, transit line-haul time, transit access time, auto line-haul cost, auto out-of-pocket cost, transit line-haul cost, and transit access cost.[g] These variables are defined as follows:

Auto in-vehicle time: Line-haul time from origin zone centroid to destination zone centroid, plus time to find a parking place in destination zone.

Auto out-of-vehicle time: Time to walk to car at origin of trip and walk from parked car to final destination.

Transit line-haul time: Time spent in the *principal* transit mode, which was determined according to an arbitrary hierarchy: rail, subway, bus, streetcar, auto. Thus, for trips involving two or more modes (for example, a feeder bus to a subway terminal and subway thereafter), only the time spent in the principal mode (*i.e.*, the subway in the above example) is taken to be line-haul time. This is an arbitrary and possibly unfortunate way to define line-haul time, but it was a decision made in preparing the data tapes for a previous study and, therefore, was not under our control.

Transit access time: Travel time spent outside the principal transit mode. It includes time spent in submodes (transit, auto or walk) going to or from principal mode stations, plus transfer time and waiting time.

[g]We also attempted to disaggregate schedule delays, but the data available were inadequate.

Auto line-haul cost: The operating cost of driving an automobile from the zone of origin to the zone of destination. It does not include ownership costs.

Auto out-of-pocket cost: Tolls plus parking charges.

Transit line-haul cost: Fare paid on the principal transit mode. Thus, the costs incurred on submodes (*e.g.*, feeder buses) are not included in the transit line-haul costs.

Transit access cost: Cost of access from the origin to the principal transit mode, plus cost of travel from the principal transit mode to the destination. It covers all trip costs except the fare on the principal travel mode.

Behavioral Assumptions and Mathematical Forms

Three basic mathematical forms of the model were tested: logarithmic, linear, and mixed log and linear. Each can be described in terms of the behavioral assumptions implied. The logarithmic model assumes that equal *relative* changes in travel times or costs evoke equal responses in travel demand. Thus it assumes, for example, that a housewife will curtail her trips to the supermarket by the same percentage amount whether her travel costs increase from ten to eleven cents or from ten to eleven dollars.

The linear model, on the other hand, focuses on *absolute* changes. Its shortcoming is that it assumes that reducing a two-hour trip by, say, ten minutes is as important as reducing a twenty-minute trip by ten minutes.

We generally prefer the mixed form to either the pure log or linear forms because, by including both terms for each variable, the effects of both relative and absolute changes in the variable are measured. Because of its greater generality, the mixed log and linear form was tested for each equation in the model. This procedure provides empirical evidence on whether absolute or relative changes in each variable are important or whether both are important. The difficulty with the mixed form is that the linear and logarithmic values of a variable are closely correlated (*i.e.*, are collinear). This makes estimation of the separate parameters difficult.

In interpreting the results of our empirical research and in comparing the estimated model parameters with our prior notions of traveler behavior, it is useful to introduce the concept of demand elasticity. For the travel demand model, elasticity is the percentage change in the number of trips demanded for a given purpose and mode in response to a 1 percent change in one of the variables giving rise to travel demand, assuming all other explanatory variables in the equation are held constant.[h] This is a particularly useful concept for comparing the sensitivity of travel demand to changes in a number of explanatory variables because elasticity is dimensionless. Thus, comparisons are not confused by the particular units in which the variables are expressed.

By convention, an effect with an elasticity of less than unity (in absolute value) is called inelastic, and one with an elasticity greater than unity (in absolute value) is called elastic. In the former case a given change in an

---

[h]Elasticity is precisely defined as

$$\eta_x = \frac{\partial N/N}{\partial x/x} = \frac{x}{N}\frac{\partial N}{\partial x}$$

where η_x is the elasticity of travel demand, N, with respect to variable x, It should be noted that, for any mathematical form except that in which all variables are expressed only in logarithms, elasticity is explanatory variable results in a less than proportionate change in demand, while in the latter case the change in demand is greater than proportionate. It is also conventional to call the elasticities with respect to the variables for the subject mode direct elasticities, and the elasticities with respect to the variables for competing modes cross-elasticities. We shall employ this terminology in the remainder of the discussion.

The use of our previously estimated demand models for the purpose of this study presents two important problems. First, any empirically derived model will be best at predicting behavior over a range of values for the variables similar to the range of values used in the estimation process. The greater the extrapolation required beyond the range of values used in the estimation, the more uncertain the prediction results. While the range of values used in estimating the model parameters is quite extensive, with round-trip line haul costs going from $.20 to $2.60 for work trips and $.20 to $1.28 for shopping trips, the observations did not include a zero fare. This problem, unfortunately, would exist for any model that was used.

The second problem arises from the use of logarithmic terms in the original demand equations. The logarithm of zero (*i.e.,* zero fare) does not exist (specifically, as x approaches zero, the logarithm of x approaches negative infinity). As a consequence, a procedure had to be selected to approximate the demand equations for a zero fare. Any procedure selected would, of necessity, be arbitrary. We elected to linearize the estimated functions through the means of the variables, *e.g.,* it was assumed that the percentage change in tripmaking due to a percentage change in fare was equal to the percentage change in fare *times* the elasticity of demand with respect to the fare evaluated at the mean fare of the sample used to obtain the estimate. We have no reason to believe that following this procedure will introduce any undue bias. In fact, in later sections of this chapter, the results of this procedure are compared with other empirical estimates of the affects of changes in the system performance variables and general consistency is observed.

Estimation Technique

The model was estimated by means of constrained multiple regression analysis, which consists of estimating parameters by minimizing the sum of squared deviations as with ordinary least squares but performing this minimization while satisfying certain prespecified conditions derived from *a priori* information. The constrained least squares regression technique used in this study states the problem as an equivalent quadratic programming problem.

One reason for the use of this method is related to the problem of unequal zone sizes. Because zones cannot generally be selected to be of equal size (expressed in terms either of area or population), the model must account for differences, particularly with respect to population. Thus a zone with twice as many people, other things being equal, is likely to produce roughly twice as

---

not equivalent to a coefficient in a regression equation. The elasticity expresses a ratio of relative changes while, for example, the coefficient in a linear model expresses a ratio of unit changes. The latter ratio is dependent on the choice of units — minutes versus hours, for example — while the former ratio is independent of the units selected.

many trips. This problem was overcome by constraining the demand elasticity with respect to the zone size variables to be unity.

The main problem, however, requiring prespecified conditions on the values of the estimated parameters is collinearity. Collinearity can be attributed either to the form of the model or to the nature of the variables. As an example of the first case, a model which contains both the linear and the logarithmic forms of a variable is necessarily subject to some degree of collinearity. The second case of collinearity occurs when trip behavior is independently influenced by two variables which show a close relationship to each other, either structurally or spuriously. Modal choice may, for instance, depend upon car ownership as well as income of the tripmakers. The structural collinearity results because car ownership itself is related to income. Because of the statistical problems resulting from collinearity, it is very difficult to assess the individual effect of collinear variables unless some additional information is provided. It is often possible to specify the sign or a reasonable range for a parameter from *a priori* knowledge or economic theory. Constrained regression allows the analyst to take advantage of this information. In such a case, this information regarding a variable is explicitly taken into account by constraining the corresponding parameters; and it then becomes possible to estimate the individual effect of the collinear variable.

Constrained regression was used to treat collinearity by imposing appropriate sign constraints on the direct elasticities and cross-elasticities of the system variables. The direct elasticities were constrained to be nonpositive and the cross-elasticities to be nonnegative.

Data

The parameters for the model were estimated using data for the Boston metropolitan area. Equations were estimated for four trip purposes: home-based work, shopping, personal business, and social-recreational trips. For a number of reasons models were not developed for school trips and nonhome-based trips.

The sample used in the study was drawn from a population of interzonal trips in the Boston area. Trip data were collected in an origin-and-destination survey conducted by Wilbur Smith and Associates in 1963 and 1964 for the Boston Regional Planning Project (BRPP). Forty-three thousand households out of a universe of 800,000 were interviewed and their trip patterns recorded. The sample levels used in the survey were 3 percent and 7 percent respectively for the zones outside and inside a cordon line represented approximately by a circumferential highway (Route 128) The corresponding expansion factors were, therefore, 33-1/3 and 14.3. For purposes of this study, the Boston area was divided into ninety-seven zones. Trip tables for each trip purpose and mode were created, showing the number of trips between each pair of zones.

Sample selection of interzonal observations was then done on the basis of a double criterion. Because we are attempting to model both the number of interzonal trips and their modal split, each zonal pair should contain both auto and public transit alternatives. Second, the number of trips represented by each observation should be large enough to overcome the high sampling variance resulting from the low sample rate in the home interview survey. It was decided to obtain preliminary samples for each trip purpose which would include all the zonal pairs for which there were at least three or six transit trips[j] (*i.e.,* one hundred or more total trips) for the given purpose observed in the home interview study.

An advantage of this sample selection criterion is that it includes only those zonal pairs for which transit travel represents a reasonable alternative to auto travel, a condition for obtaining a meaningful measure of modal cross-elasticities. On the other hand, the deletion of observations where few transit trips are made may result in some bias.

A problem with the sampling criterion is that it largely limits the data base to downtown-oriented trips, because most transit trips go downtown. This is unfortunate for several reasons. First, the number of destinations is small, which means that estimation of attraction parameters, as well as of those modal split parameters which are related to destinations, is made difficult. Second, the model is likely to predict poorly for zonal pairs where a good transit alternative does not exist. From the standpoint of this study, however, the selection of a downtown-oriented, transit-oriented sample is less serious a drawback than it would be for many studies since we are largely interested in downtown transit problems. The size of the samples used in the model estimation and the criterion for selection are summarized as follows:

Trip Purpose	Selection Criterion	Observations
Work Transit	100 or more Transit Trips	370
Work Auto[k]	100 or more Transit Trips	510
Shop	100 or more Transit or Auto Trips	75
Personal Business	100 or more Transit Trips	55
Social and Recreational	100 or more Transit Trips	77

Empirical Results

Although equations were developed for four trip purposes, only the work and shopping equations are used in this study. The shopping trip equations are

[j]The number was based on the sampling rate for the zone. The lower criterion was for the outlying zones, where the lower zonal sampling rate was used.

[k]In an attempt to make the auto work trip sample more representative, the sample was expanded to include zonal pairs for which 100 or more auto or transit trips were found. The final sample was then cut in

assumed to represent all nonwork trips, because we have more confidence in the results of the models for these two trip purposes than for the other two purposes. The estimated parameters of the personal business and social-recreational trip purposes are probably less reasonable than the parameters for work and shopping trips because of the difficulties in structuring the former models. The structuring of the social-recreation model is made difficult because two different trip purposes which are only superficially similar are grouped together. Moreover, personal business and social-recreational trips are difficult to model because the trip attraction variables are less clearly defined than they are for work and shopping trips. Most of the issues with which this study is primarily concerned involve work and shopping trips, but this is not altogether the case, so the limitations of the use of shopping trips to represent all nonwork trips should be borne in mind in evaluating our findings.

Tables 2-1 and 2-2 present the elasticities of demand for auto and transit work and shopping trips with respect to each component of travel time and cost. As noted above, the elasticities are calculated at the mean values of the variables. The equations from which these elasticities were computed are given in the appendix to this chapter, together with the estimated equations for personal business and social-recreation trips.

The results presented in Tables 2-1 and 2-2 lead to several important conclusions. First, Table 2-1 indicates that the demand for transit trips is very inelastic with respect to changes in fares. The transit fare elasticity for shopping trips is only -.323. The sum of the two fare elasticities for transit work trips is only -.19. The transit line-haul cost represents the principal mode fare while the access cost largely represents the feeder bus fare. The sum of the line-haul and access cost elasticities measures the fare elasticity if all transit trips were combination trips (i.e., involved more than one transit mode). In Boston about three-fourths of the transit users are combination riders so the aggregate fare elasticity for work trips is about -.17. These low elasticities indicate that substantial transit fare reductions cannot be counted on to stimulate transit ridership greatly. Indeed, they suggest that an increase in fares would increase transit revenues because a given fare rise would produce much less than a proportionate drop in ridership.

The second general conclusion that can be drawn from these tables is that most of the cross-elasticities are very low or zero. The zero values for these cross-elasticities should not be taken literally, of course. They are zero because the constraints were binding, not because they were estimated to be zero, and should be interpreted as a lack of evidence of a positive cross-elasticity. These low cross-elasticities indicate that it will be very difficult to entice auto travelers to use transit by lowering fares or by improving service. Indeed, the low cross-elasticities suggest that modal decisions are governed more by the socioeconomic characteristics of the traveler than by comparative times or costs of travel by the different modes, although work trips seem more likely to be diverted to transit than shopping trips, and reductions in transit travel times (especially access times) will be more consequential in this regard than

---

half by random selection. In the original study, it was necessary to estimate circumferential auto trips and this required a more representative sample for auto trips.

Table 2-1

Elasticities of Passenger Travel Demand with Respect to the Components of Travel Cost

Trip Purpose	Auto Trips Direct Elasticities		Cross-Elasticities[2]		R^2
	Auto Line-Haul	Auto Out-of-Pocket	Transit Line-Haul	Transit Access	
Work	⁻494	⁻ .071	.138	0	.41
Shopping	-.878	-1.65	0	0	.55

Trip Purpose	Transit Trips Direct Elasticities		Cross-Elasticities[2]		R^2
	Transit Line-Haul	Transit Access	Auto Line-Haul	Auto Out-of-Pocket	
Work	-.09	-.100	0	0	.35
Shopping	-.323[1]		0	0	.63

[1] The available shopping transit trip sample was unsuitable for estimating elasticities for the disaggregated cost components.

[2] The zero cross-elasticities shown in the table occurred because constrained regression analysis was used in estimating the parameters of the model and the constraints were binding for the variables for which zero cross-elasticities are shown. They were not estimated to be zero.

Table 2-2

**Elasticities of Passenger Travel Demand
with Respect to the Components of
Travel Time**

	Auto Trips			
	Direct Elasticities		Cross-Elasticities[2]	
	Auto	Auto	Transit	Transit
Trip Purpose	In-Vehicle	Out-of-Vehicle	Line-Haul	Access
Work	− .82	−1.437	0	.373
Shopping	−1.02	−1.440	.0950	0

	Transit Trips			
	Direct Elasticities		Cross-Elasticities[2]	
	Transit	Transit	Auto	Auto
Trip Purpose	Line-Haul	Access	In-Vehicle	Out-of-Vehicle
Work	−.39	−.709	0	0
Shopping		−.593[1]	0	0

[1] The available shopping transit trip sample
was unsuitable for estimating elasticities for
the disaggregated time components.

[2] The zero cross-elasticities shown in the
table occurred because constrained regression
analysis was used in estimating the paramenters
of the model and the constraints were binding
for the variables for which zero cross-
elasticities are shown. They were not
estimated to be zero.

reductions in fares. The access time cross-elasticity of .373 is about 2.5 times the fare cross-elasticity of .138 for work trips.

Third, it is very apparent from the tables that travel demand is more responsive to reductions in travel time than to reductions in fares. For shopping trips transit demand is about twice as responsive to changes in travel time as it is to changes in fares (*i.e.*, -.593 compared to -.323). For work trips, the elasticity with respect to transit access time is about 3.5 times the combined fare elasticity (-.709 compared to -.17) while the line-haul time elasticity is about double the combined fare elasticity (-.39 to -.17).

Finally, there is some evidence that transit ridership is more responsive to improvements in collection and distribution service than to increases in line-haul speeds. The transit line-haul time elasticity for work trips is only about half the access time elasticity. Unfortunately these variables were not disaggregated for shopping trips. Some indirect evidence on this point is provided, however, by the auto time elasticities. For both work and shopping trips the elasticities are greater for out-of-vehicle than for in-vehicle time. These results suggest that travelers find out-of-vehicle time more onerous than in-vehicle time, which seems reasonable. If this conclusion is accurate, it indicates that proposals for rapid transit or express bus service, which chiefly reduce line-haul time, may be less attractive to users than improvements in the collection and distribution service. All of these conclusions are, of course, subject to the qualifications stated earlier regarding the transit data and the sample, as well as qualifications about the statistical reliability of the estimates.

Statistical Reliability

In comparing the model presented here with those currently in use, some discussion is in order regarding the statistical reliability of the estimates. In particular, we often look at measures of goodness of fit such as the estimated coefficient of multiple determination (R^2) as an indication of the degree of success in explaining the variations in traffic movements in the base data. We are accustomed to finding very high levels of R^2 for trip generation and attraction equations, suggesting that a high proportion of traffic movements have been explained. But because these high correlation statistics represent only the number of trips leaving or arriving in a zone, they may be extremely deceptive when our interest is in the origin/destination pattern of trips.

In our model the values of R^2 are substantially lower than those generally reported. The values obtained for the four equations range from 0.35 to 0.63. In comparing these correlation statistics with those generally reported, however, it is necessary to recognize that our results show the percentage of zone-to-zone traffic explained, whereas the correlation statistics reported for conventional models relate only to the number of trips leaving or arriving in a zone. It is obviously more difficult to predict interzonal movements than the total number of trips leaving or arriving in a zone. Therefore, lower values of R^2 for our model are not surprising. It should also be pointed out that the values of R^2 obtained with these models are not unusual in economic cross-section analysis.

It is not unreasonable to believe that if values of R^2 were obtained for zone-to-zone trips for the existing models, they would be of lower magnitude than those found in our study, particularly if corrections are made for the number of degrees of freedom. The data used in this study, though not very satisfactory, are no worse than those used in other traffic demand studies and there is reason to believe they were used at least as efficiently as in other demand models. This suggests that the amount of uncertainty in the estimates of interzonal traffic flows in the existing studies may be substantially higher than has generally been recognized.

The high level of residual error in estimating the total choice mechanism (as opposed to a single aspect) should be regarded as a danger signal by the planner. The result implies high uncertainty in our predictions of the effects of changes in the transportation system. When account is taken of sampling errors and errors in predicting independent variables, in addition to the generally low correlation statistics, it is clear that the uncertainty in predicting future origin and destination traffic movements is very great indeed. The planner must therefore be extremely cautious in his decisions and explicitly recognize that his evaluations are subject to this uncertainty.

Corroborating Evidence

In view of the many qualifications attached to the results given above, it is useful to compare briefly these results with the findings of other relevant traffic demand studies. The two most systematic and comprehensive studies of modal choice are those of Traffic Research Corporation (TRC, now Peak, Marwick, Livingston & Company), prepared for the National Capital Transportation Agency, and the CRA model described above. These models used quite different procedures, and both were hampered by the quality of the available data, yet they yielded fairly consistent results.

Elaboration of the details of the TRC model would be a diversion here. Of relevance, though, are the sensitivity tests subsequently conducted on the model by the Bureau of Public Roads.[1] These tests entailed specifying particular changes in price or service and calculating the results, aggregating over all subclasses of work trips. The most obvious conclusion to be drawn from these tests is the almost complete insensitivity of transit's share of the market to such transit system performance variables as its fare or times, and the much greater weight that the "distribution" or "trip end" phase of the total automobile trip had in the results — parking time and costs, and walking time. For example, for a $.15 addition to prevailing transit fares ($.35 prevailing), the predicted effect on travel was a 5 percent reduction, implying a price elasticity of -.12. For a doubling of fares, travel declined by only 7.8 percent. The authors who made this examination of the TRC model indicated that the extent of variation in the

[1]Arthur B. Sosslan and Arthur J. Balek, "Evaluation of a New Modal Split Procedure", *Highway Research Record*, No. 88, Highway Research Board, 1965.

fare structure really did not permit inferences to be made with any reliability as to the effects of alternative fares. Nevertheless, these results are quite consistent with the findings of the CRA model as to the low fare elasticity as well as to the low cross-elasticities between modes.

Other qualitative evidence on transit demand, although of a less systematic nature than the two modal split models discussed above, lend support to their general implications. For example, for some years now the transit industry has used a formula (the Simpson and Curtin formula) which states that each 1 percent increase in fares will cause a 1/3 percent decrease in riders. This implies a fare elasticity of -.33, a magnitude similar to the fare elasticities of -.17 and -.32 presented in Table 2-1.

Also, a number of case studies are of interest. The Boston experience in adjusting its fares in October 1961 is a case worth noting. Prior to the change, Boston had a flat $.20 transit fare and a free transfer to feeder bus. There was, thus, extensive use of feeder buses on one-half to two-thirds of a mile distances to the rapid transit stations. The change involved instituting a $.10 addition to the combination of transit-bus and streetcar fares, reducing local surface fares from $.15 to $.10, and eliminating the $.05 transfer from one surface bus to another.

The result based on the MBTA's turnstile counts at the Central Business District (CBD) stations was a decline from May 8, 1961, to May 7, 1962, from 171,035 to 152,365 or 11 percent on weekdays. On Saturdays the decline was slightly larger, 19 percent, from 107,933 to 87,675. (Sunday data contain some odd fluctuations, and are considered unreliable.) The peak load point counts on the streetcar lines showed a 16 percent decline in the peak-hour, two-way traffic, and a 20 percent decline the remainder of the day. Only incomplete data exist on the feeder bus lines, but they indicate a decrease of 10 to 25 percent on weekdays (for two-way totals), 20 to 35 percent on Saturdays, and 25 to 50 percent on Sundays (measured by peak load point counts by the MBTA).

Basically the change resulted in about a 10 percent reduction in total peak transit travel and about twice that amount of a reduction in feeder bus use. Obviously some 10 percent chose to walk or go by car in view of the $.10 fare on feeder buses. The response of travelers to this change in feeder bus fares is a useful check on the CRA demand model, where the effects should be reflected largely in the parameter for "access" cost, all costs spent prior to the final line-haul vehicle trip. As mentioned above, in Boston a high percentage of rapid transit riders are "combination" bus-rail riders. In the case of transit work trips, the "access" cost elasticity was about -.10 and was not much different for nonwork trips (the value varied from -.04 to -.37). The model fitted with the 1966 cross-section sample thus is surprisingly accurate in modeling the 1961 experience.

Another interesting case is the Massachusetts Mass Transportation Commission (MTC) demonstration project on the Boston commuter railroads. On the rail lines of the Boston and Maine Railroad which received a 24 to 30 percent fare decrease (but no service change), peak-hour riding increased only 2 percent, even accounting for the declining trend evidenced after the return to normal fares. These lines were rush-hour only, one or two train lines. On the New Haven, fare decreases of 9 to 13 percent produced mixed results, mostly negligible; where increases in riding of up to 12 percent did occur, they continued after the fare returned to normal, so that ascribing the increase to the fare change would be questionable. This evidence of the demonstration project thus also supports the very low price elasticities suggested by the CRA and the TRC models.

A final case study worth considering is the recent New York City experience.[m] In July 1966 the basic subway and bus fare in New York City was increased from \$.15 to \$.20, or 33 percent. Subway ridership declined about 2.5 percent during the year following the fare increase (fiscal year 1967), while bus ridership declined about 10 percent. Thus, the fare elasticity implied by the bus experience is about -.33, the same elasticity implied by the Simpson and Curtin formula and almost the same elasticity given by the CRA model for transit shopping trips. The subway fare elasticity implied by the New York experience is about -.08, somewhat lower than the elasticities found in the CRA model, but nevertheless providing strong support for the low fare elasticities found in the CRA model.

Appendix

Tables A-1 through A-8 give estimates of travel demand equations for the four trip purposes and two modes. Table A-9 gives the means of the system characteristic variables for work and shopping trips.

---

[m]A detailed discussion of the recent New York experience is given in *The Effect of the Fare Increase of July, 1966 on the Number of Passengers Carried in the New York City Transit System*, by W. Lassow (paper presented at the annual meeting of the Highway Research Board, January 1968).

Table A-1

Work Auto Trips

Dependent Variable = $\dfrac{\text{Number of Directed Work Round Trips by Auto}}{\begin{bmatrix}\text{Employed labor} \\ \text{force in zone} \\ \text{of residence}\end{bmatrix} \times \begin{bmatrix}\text{Employment in zone of} \\ \text{work as a proportion of} \\ \text{total employment in the} \\ \text{region}\end{bmatrix}}$

Independent Variables:

Description of Variable	Coefficient
Constant	-31.0250
Ln (In-vehicle time − auto)	-1.7973
Ln (Median income of households and unrelated individuals in zone of residence	6.1168
Median income of households and unrelated individuals in zone of residence	$.0020$
Ln (Out-of-pocket costs − auto)	$-.1552$
Ln (Line-haul costs − transit)	$.3034$
Ln (Out-of-vehicle time − auto)	-3.1387
Ln (Access time − transit)	$.8153$
Ln (Line-haul cost − auto)	-1.0793
Employment density in zone of work	$-.0063$
Ln (Number of cars per capita in zone of residence)	$.0270$
Number of cars per capita in zone of residence	13.2677

Table A-1 (continued)

Variables Introduced in the Model
Which Take a Zero Coefficient:

Description of Variable

In-vehicle time — auto

Ln (Line-haul time — transit)

Line-haul time — transit

Out-of-pocket costs — auto

Line-haul cost — transit

Out-of-vehicle time — auto

Access time — transit

Line-haul cost — auto

Ln (Access cost — transit)

Access cost — transit

Form of the Model:

$N = (\alpha X + \beta \ln X) Y$ where: $\eta_X =$ elasticity of demand with respect to variable X

$\eta_X = \dfrac{\alpha X + \beta}{N} Y$

$N =$ number of trips

$X =$ independent variables

$Y = \begin{bmatrix} \text{employed labor} \\ \text{force in zone} \\ \text{of residence} \end{bmatrix} \times \begin{bmatrix} \text{employment in zone of work} \\ \text{as a proportion of total} \\ \text{employment in the region} \end{bmatrix}$

$\alpha, \beta =$ estimated parameters

Table A-2

Work Transit Trips

Dependent Variable = Ln (number of
directed work round trips by transit)

Independent Variables:

Description of Variable	Coefficient
Constant	−12.158232
Ln (Employed labor force in zone of residence)	1.000000
Ln (Employment in zone of work as a proportion of total employment in region)	1.000000
Ln (Line-haul time − transit)	− 0.190862
Line-haul time − transit	− 0.005843
Ln (Median income of households and unrelated individuals in zone of residence)	1.144006
Ln (Line-haul cost − transit)	.036214
Line-haul cost − transit	− 0.002362
Ln (Access time − transit)	.462262
Access Time − transit	− .025288
Access cost − transit	− .005095
Ln (Number of cars per capita in zone of residence)	− 1.163856
Number of cars per capita in zone of residence	1.777146

Variables Introduced in the Model Which Take a Zero Coefficient:

Ln (In-vehicle time − auto)

In-vehicle time − auto

Table A-2 (continued)

Variables Introduced in the Model Which
Take a Zero Coefficient (continued):

Description of Variable

Ln (Out-of-pocket costs — auto)

Out-of-pocket costs — auto

Out-of-vehicle time — auto

Total out-of-vehicle time — auto

Ln (Access cost — transit)

Ln (Line-haul cost — auto)

Line-haul cost — auto

Form of Model:

$$N = X^\alpha e^{\beta X} \qquad \eta_X = \text{elasticity of demand with respect to variable } X$$

$$\eta_X = \alpha + \beta X \qquad N = \text{number of trips}$$

$$X = \text{independent variables}$$

$$\alpha, \beta = \text{estimated parameters}$$

Table A-3

Shopping Auto Trips

Dependent Variable = Ln (number of
directed shopping round trips by auto)

Independent Variables:

Description of Variable	Coefficient
Constant	−2.733324
Ln (Number of households in zone of residence)	1.000000
Ln (Employment in retail trade in zone of destination as a proportion of total regional employment in retail trade)	1.000000
Ln (In-vehicle time − auto)	− .081710
In-vehicle time − auto	− .024824
Ln (Line-haul time − transit)	.095003
Ln (Median income of households and unrelated individuals)	.304834
Median income of households and unrelated individuals	− .000029
Ln (Out-of-pocket cost − auto)	− .853097
Out-of-pocket cost − auto	− .050591
Ln (Out-of-vehicle time − auto)	−1.439808
Ln (line haul cost − auto)	− .878061
Ln (Number of persons per household in zone of residence)	−3.048188
Number of persons per household in zone of residence	.583934
Ln (Density of employment in retail trade in zone of destination)	−.759571

Table A-3 (continued)

Independent Variables (continued):

Description of Variable	Coefficient
Density of employment in retail trade in zone of destination	.086956
Ln (Number of cars per capita in zone of residence)	−2.341933
Number of cars per capita in zone of residence	15.303761

Variables Introduced in the Model Which Take a Zero Coefficient:

Line-haul time − transit

Ln (Line-haul cost − transit)

Line-haul cost − transit

Out-of-vehicle time − auto

Ln (Access time − transit)

Access time − transit

Line-haul cost − auto

Ln (Access cost − transit)

Access cost − transit

Form of the Model:

$$N = X^{\alpha} e^{\beta X} \qquad \text{where:} \quad \eta_X = \text{elasticity of demand with respect to variable } X$$

$$\eta_X = \alpha + \beta X$$

$$N = \text{number of trips}$$

$$X = \text{independent variable}$$

$$\alpha, \beta = \text{estimated parameters}$$

Table A-4

Shopping Transit Trips

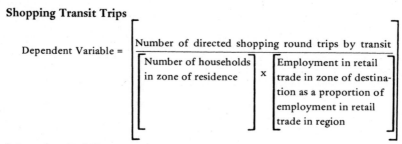

Dependent Variable = $\left[\dfrac{\text{Number of directed shopping round trips by transit}}{\left[\begin{array}{l}\text{Number of households}\\ \text{in zone of residence}\end{array}\right] \times \left[\begin{array}{l}\text{Employment in retail}\\ \text{trade in zone of destina-}\\ \text{tion as a proportion of}\\ \text{employment in retail}\\ \text{trade in region}\end{array}\right]}\right]$

Independent Variables:

Variable Number	Description of Variable	Coefficient
	Constant	−1.976884
	Ln (Total time − transit)	−.593240
	Ln (Median income of households in zone of residence)	−.048626
	Ln (Total cost − transit)	−.323692
	Ln (Number of persons per household)	2.483299
	Ln (Density of employment in retail trade)	.030759
	Ln (Employment in personal business activities in zone of destination as a proportion of employment in personal business in region)	−.739325

NOTE: This model is unconstrained.

Table A-4 (continued)

Form of the Model:

$$N = X^{\alpha}Y$$

$$\eta_X = \alpha$$

where:

η_X = elasticity of demand with respect to variable X

N = number of trips

X = independent variable

$Y = \begin{bmatrix} \text{number of households} \\ \text{in zone of residence} \end{bmatrix} \times \begin{bmatrix} \text{employment in retail trade} \\ \text{in zone of destination as a} \\ \text{proportion of total em-} \\ \text{ployment in retail trade in} \\ \text{region} \end{bmatrix}$

α, β = estimated parameters

Table A-5

Personal Business Auto Trips

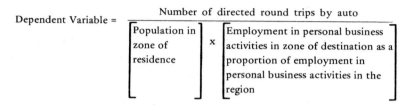

Dependent Variable = $\dfrac{\text{Number of directed round trips by auto}}{\begin{bmatrix}\text{Population in} \\ \text{zone of} \\ \text{residence}\end{bmatrix} \times \begin{bmatrix}\text{Employment in personal business} \\ \text{activities in zone of destination as a} \\ \text{proportion of employment in} \\ \text{personal business activities in the} \\ \text{region}\end{bmatrix}}$

Independent Variables:

Description of Variable	Coefficient
Constant	−.8295
Ln (In-vehicle time − auto)	−.6949
Ln (Median income of household and related individuals)	.5209
Median income of households and related individuals	−.0002
Ln (Out-of-pocket cost − auto)	−.1481
Ln (Out-of-vehicle time − auto)	−.0174
Out-of-vehicle time − auto	−.0401
Ln (Line-haul cost − auto)	−.1241
Ln (Number of persons per household)	−3.6955
Number of persons per houseshold	1.5928
Employment density in personal business activity in zone of destination	−.0011
Ln (Number of cars per capita in zone of residence)	.0542
Number of car per capita in zone of residence	2.5307

Table A-5 (continued)

Variables Introduced in the Model Which
Take a Zero Coefficient:

Description of Variable

In-vehicle time — auto

Ln (Line-haul time — transit)

Line-haul time — transit

Out-of-pocket cost — auto

Ln (Line-haul cost — transit)

Line-haul cost — transit

Ln (Access time — transit)

Access time — transit

Line-haul cost — auto

Ln (Access cost — transit)

Access cost — transit

Form of the Model:

$N = (\alpha X + \beta \, lnX) \, Y$ where: η_X = elasticity of demand with respect to variable X

$$\eta_X = \frac{\alpha X + \beta}{N} Y$$

N = number of trips

X = independent variable

$Y = \begin{bmatrix} \text{population in} \\ \text{zone of} \\ \text{residence} \end{bmatrix} \times \begin{bmatrix} \text{employment in personal} \\ \text{business activities in} \\ \text{zone of destination} \\ \text{as a proportion of} \\ \text{employment in personal} \\ \text{business in the region} \end{bmatrix}$

α, β = estimated parameters

Table A-6

Personal Business Transit Trips

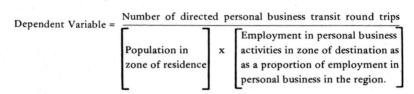

Dependent Variable = $\dfrac{\text{Number of directed personal business transit round trips}}{\left[\begin{array}{c}\text{Population in}\\\text{zone of residence}\end{array}\right] \times \left[\begin{array}{l}\text{Employment in personal business}\\\text{activities in zone of destination as}\\\text{as a proportion of employment in}\\\text{personal business in the region.}\end{array}\right]}$

Independent Variables:

Description of Variable	Coefficient
Constant	−4.067807
Ln (Line-haul time − transit)	−.196589
Ln (In-vehicle time − auto)	.025189
Ln (Median income of household plus unrelated individuals)	.645979
Median income of household plus unrelated individuals	−.000042
Ln (Out-of-pocket cost − auto)	.031538
Ln (Access cost − transit)	−.020714
Ln (Line-haul cost − auto)	.093999
Ln (Number of persons per household)	2.662359
Number of persons per household	−1.014880
Ln (Density of employment in personal business activities)	−.196866
Density of employment in personal business activities	.013668
Ln (Number of cars per capita)	.115560
Number of cars per capita	−1.444498

Table A-6 (continued)

Variables Introduced in the Model Which
Take a Zero Coefficient:

Description of Variable
Line-haul time — transit
In-vehicle time — auto
Ln (Line-haul cost — transit)
Line-haul cost — transit
Out-of-pocket cost — auto
Ln (Access time — transit)
Access time — transit
Ln (Out-of-vehicle time — auto)
Out-of-vehicle time — auto
Access cost — transit
Line-haul cost — auto

Form of the Model:

$N = (\alpha X + \beta \ln X) Y$ where: $\quad \eta_X$ = elasticity of demand with respect to variable X

$$\eta_X = \frac{\alpha X + \beta}{N} Y$$

N = number of trips

X = independent variable

$Y = \begin{bmatrix} \text{population} \\ \text{in zone of} \\ \text{residence} \end{bmatrix} \times \begin{bmatrix} \text{employment in personal business} \\ \text{activities in zone of destination} \\ \text{as a proportion of employment in} \\ \text{personal business in the region.} \end{bmatrix}$

α, β = estimated parameters

Table A-7

Social and Recreational Auto Trips

Dependent Variable = (Number of directed social and recreational auto round trips)

Independent Variables:

Description of Variable	Coefficient
Constant	4.500665
Ln (Population in zone of origin)	1.000000
Ln (Population in zone of destination as a proportion of of total population in region)	1.000000
Ln (Difference in median incomes of households and unrelated individuals between zone of origin and zone of destination)	−0.113799
Difference in median incomes of households and unrelated individuals between zone of origin and zone of destination	0.000182
Ln (In-vehicle time − auto)	−1.131201
Ln (Out-of-pocket cost − auto)	−0.015423
Ln (Line-haul cost − transit)	0.136115
Line-haul cost − transit	0.002184
Ln (Out-of-vehicle time − auto)	−0.861877
Ln (Line-haul cost − auto)	0.011624
Line-haul cost − auto	−0.049387
Access cost − transit	0.010048
Employment in social and recreational activities in zone of destination as a proportion of total employment in social and recreational activities in the region	13.314361

Table A-7 (continued)

Variables Introduced in the Model Which
Take a Zero Coefficient:

Description of Variable

In-vehicle time — auto

Ln (Line-haul time — transit)

Line-haul time — transit

Out-of-pocket — auto

Out-of-vehicle time — auto

Ln (Access time — transit)

Access time — transit

Ln (Access cost — transit)

Form of the Model:

$$N = X^{\alpha} e^{\beta X}$$ where: η_X = elasticity of demand with respect to variable X

$$\eta_X = \alpha + \beta X$$ N = number of trips

X = independent variable

α, β = estimated parameters

Table A-8

Social and Recreational Transit Trips

Dependent Variable = $\dfrac{\text{Number of Directed Social and Recreational Transit Round Trips}}{\left[\begin{array}{l}\text{Population in} \\ \text{zone of origin}\end{array}\right] \times \left[\begin{array}{l}\text{Population in zone of destination as a} \\ \text{proportion of total population in region}\end{array}\right]}$

Independent Variables:

Description of Variable	Coefficient
Constant	0.772761
Ln (Difference in median incomes of households and unrelated individuals between zone of origin and zone of destination)	−0.175305
Difference in median incomes of households and unrelated individuals between zone of origin and zone of destination	0.000470
Ln (Line-haul time − transit)	0.101386
Line-haul time − transit	−0.025346
Ln (Line-haul cost − transit)	0.230423
Line-haul cost − transit	−0.011521
Out-of-pocket cost − auto	0.013090
Ln (Out-of-vehicle time − auto)	0.155641
Ln (Access cost − transit)	−0.163730
Employment in social and recreational activities in zone of destination as a proportion of total employment in social and recreational activities in the region	9.468327

Table A-8 (continued)

Variables Introduced in the Model Which
Take a Zero Coefficient:

Description of Variable

Ln (In-vehicle time — auto)

In-vehicle time —auto

Ln (Out-of-pocket cost — auto)

Ln (Access time — transit)

Access time — transit

Out-of-vehicle time — auto

Access cost — transit

Ln (Line-haul cost — auto)

Line-haul cost — auto

Form of the Model:

$N = (\alpha X + \beta \ln X)\, Y$ where: η_X = elasticity of demand with respect to variable X

$$\eta_X = \frac{\alpha + \beta X}{N}\, Y$$

N = number of trips

X = independent variable

$Y = \begin{bmatrix} \text{population in} \\ \text{zone of origin} \end{bmatrix} \times \begin{bmatrix} \text{population in zone of destination as a proportion of total population in region} \end{bmatrix}$

α, β = estimated parameters

Table A-9

**Means of System Characteristic
Variables for Interzonal Exchanges in
the Boston Area Sample**

Description of Variable	Transit Sample	Auto Sample	Shopping	Personal Business	Social and Recreational
Line-haul time — transit (minutes)	34.69	35.24	27.13	21.62	24.51
Access time — transit (minutes)	46.84	52.58	47.76	42.11	39.93
In-vehicle time — auto (minutes)	54.43	49.73	37.15	39.00	34.23
Out-of-vehicle time — auto (minutes)	5.40	5.15	5.44	6.00	6.22
Line-haul cost — transit (cents)	56.06	51.69	48.95	42.53	43.78
Access cost — Transit (cents)	20.01	22.58	15.43	13.21	12.78
Line-haul cost — auto (cents)	36.88	34.32	20.70	17.74	12.36
Out-of-pocket cost — auto (cents)	18.31	8.35	16.35	12.96	7.97

3

Implications of a Program of Free Transit Service on System Performance and Technology

System Performance

To evaluate a program of free transit, an analysis is needed of the effects of eliminating fare collection on system performance. A full-scale system analysis is required to do this properly. Account must be made of the feedback between system operations, service, and the rider market, over both the short and long run. Although a full-scale simulation effort was precluded by the time limitations of the study, it will be useful to outline and describe some of the principal effects stemming from a program of free transit.

We shall examine, to the extent possible, the effect of free transit on transit operations and in turn on passenger service and ridership. Elimination of fare collection will, of course, have different effects on different technological systems or transit operations. That is, for a local bus service in which the fares are collected from passengers as they board the bus, the effects will be somewhat different than they will be for rail transit service or bus service with centralized fare collection.

For local bus service, in which the driver also must serve as the fare collector, the institution of free transit would have several immediate short-run effects. First, the bus will be able to load and unload passengers more quickly, because people will not have to spend time hunting for change, and since both front and back doors can be used for loading and unloading. Bus operations will also be made more efficient in the short run because the driver can concentrate on driving and on opening and closing the doors. Both effects will tend to cause travel time *and* the overall bus trip time to be reduced, permitting higher utilization of labor and buses. Maintenance of fare collection equipment can also be eliminated. Finally, the bus can be more fully loaded because people will spread out more freely and move to the back of the bus, reducing queueing and delays in rush hours.

Over the longer run the elimination of fare collection could (other things held constant) result in a reduction of both labor force and rolling stock and could pave the way for some significant changes in bus design. For example, buses might be designed with better door locations (such as doors spaced at the one-fourth points of the passenger portion of the bus). In addition, the elimination of robbery, and threats on the driver's life could eventually result in reduced operator wages.

For either the usual rail transit service or bus service with centralized fare collection, the advantages would be less pronounced than local bus operations and of somewhat different character. Where a centralized fare collection system is used, passenger trip times have improved because the time needed to wait in line, insert fares, get change, and so forth, has been transferred to the waiting time from the line-haul time portions of the trip. The transit operation would be cheaper in the short run, however, because fare collection, auditing, etc., could be eliminated (at least to some extent, depending of course on institutional constraints). It would not be necessary to buy and maintain fare collection equipment. Insurance and operator wages might also be lowered because of the reduction in the possibility of robbery. Over the long run the size of the terminal and its required real estate could be somewhat reduced with a resulting reduction in costs. Note that elimination of the fare collection process from an already centralized fare collection transit operation would not affect the enroute trip times of the transit vehicles themselves. Therefore, with the introduction of free transit, passengers using that kind of service would not find their delay reduced to the same extent as those using noncentralized fare collection transit services.

Changes in price or in service characteristics (such as improvements in loading or unloading time as a consequence of eliminating fare collection) will of necessity have repercussions on the demand for transit service. Due primarily to two factors, the result of an increase in demand will be longer travel times, as long as there are no equipment or scheduling changes. First, the probability of having to stop at any one stop is increased as the number of riders goes up. The significance of this effect will depend on route density, number of stops, average travel speed, etc. For each stop, however, there is a fixed time associated with decelerating, opening the doors, closing the doors, and accelerating back to normal travel speed. Secondly, the aggregate loading and unloading time increases as the number of riders getting on or off at a given stop increases.

The full extent of changes in transit operations and passenger service stemming from free transit can only be determined by examining the details of a particular system, the route structure, the pattern of passenger usage (*i.e.,* length of passenger runs and loads at different stops), the specifics of the transit operation and technology, and so forth. However, short of this precise treatment, it does seem worthwhile to provide some rough estimates of the scale of the changes which might be anticipated in, say, an average situation, to discuss some of the data that impinge on these situations, and to sketch out the feedbacks that seem likely to occur.

For local bus services, it is not clear whether total travel times will improve because of the decreased loading and unloading times achieved by eliminating fare collection, or whether they will deteriorate because of a heavier volume of usage. Some estimates of the time required for passengers to load and unload onto buses under different conditions of fare collection are shown in Table 3-1.

Table 3-1

Passenger Headways On and Off Buses

Condition	Item	Time (seconds)
Unloading	Little hand baggage and paracels; few transfers	1½ - 2½
	Moderate hand baggare or many transfers	2½ - 4
	Considerable baggage from racks	4 - 6
Loading	Single coin or token fare box	2 - 3
	Odd-penny cash fares	3 - 4
	Multi-zone fares:	
	Prepurch. tickets and regis. by driver	4 - 6
	Cash including regis. by driver	6 - 8

Source: *Highway Capacity Manual,* 1965, Highway Research Board Special Report No. 87, Washington, D.C., 1965, p. 346

In order to give some perspective to these figures, the graphical display of a sample of loading and unloading times for trolley and diesel bus lines for a situation in which fares were collected is shown in Figure 3-1.[a] Looking at the figure, one is struck by the variability of the process. For example, when three persons are involved, the average time per person varies from about one to five seconds. Comparison of the unloading with the loading times in Table 3-1 suggests that there is apparently some increase in overall time which is directly attributable to fare collection. It is small, however, and highly variable because it is very much a function of the fare charged and the collection mechanisms as well as the total number of passengers being picked up or discharged. In general, for those cases where change must typically be made — such as where the fare is $.12 — fare collection will take longer. Securing transfers may also increase the time required for the fare collection process. It is likely, however, that fare collection is not as important in the overall time requirements as a number of other variables, such as floor level loading, number of doors, platform layout and configuration. Some of these factors are, of course, associated with fare collection under present-day technology (the location of doors for example).

The importance of each of the factors mentioned above in local bus operations can be appreciated more fully by looking at an example situation.

Suppose that a four-mile bus line typically picks up sixty passengers over twenty possible bus stops. At twenty-five miles per hour the trip would take 9.6 minutes if there were no stops. However, the acceleration and deceleration at each stop requires approximately eleven seconds additional time. If currently fifteen of the twenty potential stops have to be made, this amounts to a total of 2.7 minutes additional time. Time for loading the sixty passengers with fare collection, assuming three seconds per passenger, is three minutes. Total time is therefore 15.3 minutes for the run.

If this bus line has a 20 percent increase in demand because of the reduction in fares, and if it is assumed that eighteen of the twenty stops must now be made, the time spent stopping will rise to 3.3 minutes. If loading and unloading time is assumed to drop to two seconds per passenger on the average, due to elimination of fare collection, the new loading and unloading time for seventy-two passengers would be 2.4 minutes and the total travel time would still be 15.3 minutes.

It is conceivable in other words that there could be either an increase or a decrease in travel time but the net change is likely to be small. Under larger assumed differences in loading and unloading rates with and without fare collection and under smaller assumed increases in demand, the elimination of fare collection would show positive time savings, while the reverse would show an increase in travel time. Net time savings should attract even more riders while net time losses should somewhat diminish the gains in ridership arising from the fare decreases. The typical situation, however, would probably be more people riding local buses with about the same travel time. This conclusion assumes that bus capacities are not challenged by the increase in ridership.

If capacities are strained by the increase in ridership, the situation becomes

---

[a]These observations were made by CRA for the purpose of this study.

more complicated. Figure 3-1 shows the substantial increase in loading and unloading time which takes place when the bus is full. The total loading and unloading time for eight people goes up to ninety seconds, or more than eleven seconds per person. Thus, if bus capacities are strained, there is likely to be a sizeable net increase in trip times, caused both by the increase in ridership and the substantially increased loading and unloading time per rider.

In the above example, if additional bus capacity is added so that load factors are held roughly constant, sixty passengers will again be served and loading and unloading time per passenger will be two seconds. Thus, total travel time will be 14.3 minutes, a reduction of one minute. The reduction occurs because with the increased number of buses we assume that only sixty passengers per bus will be boarded and discharged and only fifteen stops will need to be made. Moreover, the additional buses will reduce the headway between buses so the time spent waiting for a bus will decrease. These two factors will reduce the overall trip time, resulting in an additional stimulus to ridership. Hence, to hold load factors constant an additional increase in capacity would be needed. In summary, for bus operations the elimination of fares is likely to result in: (1) increased ridership and very little change in travel times when bus capacities are not strained; and (2) an even greater increase in ridership and reduced overall trip times when additional capacity is added to accommodate the added passengers.

For the usual rapid transit service or for bus service with centralized fare collection, the net results would be much the same, although the impact on each of the components of trip time would be smaller. The elimination of fares would eliminate the time to get a token or fare and to pass through the turnstile (unless the turnstiles were preserved to measure the traffic). The average time savings per person would probably be about the same for rush and nonrush hours. The elimination of queueing during rush hours would increase the average peak-hour time savings, but during the rush hour a high percentage of riders have tokens and this would reduce the average time savings per person during those hours. The time savings per person would be smaller than on buses because the centralized operations are more efficient and would take place in part during time that would otherwise be spent waiting for a train; thus, only a portion of this time saving on the average would be a net reduction in trip time. As with bus operations, the reduced fare would increase ridership so that reduced boarding times per person, resulting from the elimination of the time taken to get a token, would be offset by the need to board more passengers. Platform boarding with numerous doorways is quite efficient so the larger number of passengers would probably not greatly increase loading and unloading time per trip. As with buses, it is probably reasonable to assume that the savings and increases in time would about offset each other. Thus, the net result of the elimination of fares would be an increase in ridership with about the same trip time, as long as no additional capacity is added to accommodate the increase in riders.

If an increase in capacity were required, headways would be reduced, thus reducing overall trip time and further stimulating usage. The reduction in

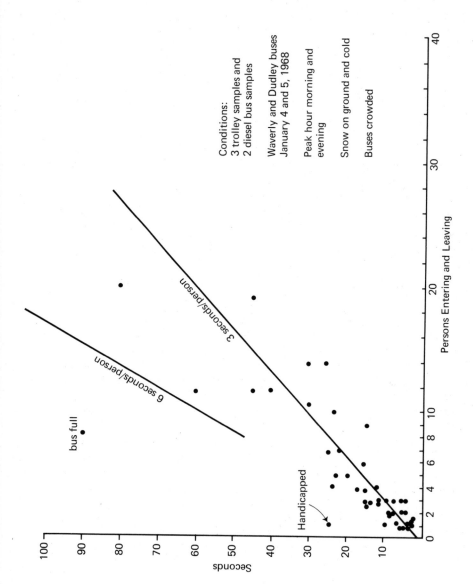

Figure 3-1   Bus loading and unloading times.

headway time would probably be smaller for rapid transit operations than for buses because the existing rush-hour headways in rapid transit systems are generally shorter than bus headways.

Up to this point we have discussed only the impact of the elimination of fares on the performance of the transit system. It is also interesting to speculate on the likely impact of free fares on the performance of the highway system. The demand model discussed in Chapter 3 shows that a reduction in fares or an improvement in transit travel times (especially access times) would divert some auto travelers to transit. The cross-elasticities are quite low, suggesting that the reduction in auto travel would be modest, even for sizeable changes in fares or transit travel times. Nevertheless, the modest reductions in auto traffic might significantly reduce rush-hour congestion.

The way in which this could occur is as follows. There is a sharp burst of auto traffic when work lets out around 5:00 P.M. In some cases, this initial burst exceeds the flow capacity of the system, causing severe congestion. The system as a whole could carry more vehicles if it could be prevented from breaking down. This is the theory of ramp metering which will be discussed later. Diversion to transit of a small portion of this initial burst of traffic could work in a way analogous to ramp metering, enabling the highway system to operate without breaking down. In this case the highway system could and probably would end up carrying more auto traffic in total than it would without the diversion to transit of some of the initial activity, because an increased proportion of the travelers who follow the initial burst of activity would choose to travel by auto if the congestion caused by the initial burst were reduced or eliminated.

Technology

It would appear that the elimination of the fare would not substantially increase transit usage. The price elasticities are quite low, and although the time elasticities are higher, the reduction in travel times resulting from the elimination of fare collection will probably be small. This raises the question of what changes in technology might be employed to improve transit operations to make them more appealing to travelers.

Two courses of action come to mind as prescriptive alternates to free public transit. The first is to improve service on the existing lines; the second is to extend the service geographically so that a greater portion of the urban area is served.

There are a number of ways in which service may be improved. Perhaps the most direct is improvement in schedule frequency. By using more vehicles the interarrival time is reduced, which shortens the individual customer's wait, increases the probability of his getting a seat, and allows him to arrive at his destination nearer to his preferred arrival time. Waiting for a bus may account for a considerable portion of total travel time, therefore, in many cases this single improvement in service may be sufficient to attract many customers, particularly those who already use the system occasionally.

Another way in which service can be improved is to decrease line-haul travel times. For vehicles operating between the extremes of the system the total travel time is very long, primarily because of stopping, loading, and unloading times. One method of reducing these times is an express bus system. Under this system, a transit vehicle begins a run in the pickup and delivery mode in the "home" area. Once it is full, it proceeds to the first line-haul station. Thereafter it runs an express service to a selected set of line-haul stations or transfer points. When it finally arrives at the destination area, it may once again revert to pickup and delivery mode. The same type of service may be furnished by two separate vehicles, one serving the pickup and delivery function, the other the line-haul function. A combination feeder bus-rail rapid transit system is an example of this latter service. However, the additional time required to transfer may, in part, defeat the higher speeds obtainable.

Achieving high line-haul speeds appears to be a problem in some metropolitan areas, particularly those without rail rapid transit, but there are two ways in which it may be accomplished. The first is to provide a separate right-of-way for buses in congested areas. In many ways this amounts to the construction of a bus rapid transit system. This is of course very expensive, but less expensive than rail rapid transit and considerably more flexible, because buses can also use local streets or high-speed highways for those areas which are not congested. A bus rapid transit system provides considerably more flexibility in dealing with planning uncertainties. In Chapter 2, we stressed the high residual errors in modeling existing travel patterns and emphasized the considerable uncertainties involved in forecasting future traffic flows. Forecasting errors are certain to occur and they are likely to be large. Because bus routes can be quickly and easily changed, compared to rail rapid transit systems, bus rapid transit is considerably more desirable in designing for an uncertain future than is rail rapid transit.

A second possibility is the use of exclusive bus lanes on existing expressways. This appears to be somewhat difficult to achieve and inefficient in the use of expressway space unless there is a very large bus flow to justify the exclusive use of an entire lane.

What may be more practical is ramp metering of the expressway with bus priority in the ramp queue. The philosophy of ramp metering runs as follows. An express highway where traffic volumes exceed capacity will eventually break down. When this happens, the result is deleterious for all vehicles caught in the system. The number of vehicles the system as a whole could accommodate is increased if breakdown could be prevented. By monitoring an express highway, incipient problem conditions can be identified before they become widespread. By metering traffic at the entrance ramps, problem conditions can be avoided. Metering would therefore smooth the flow of vehicles onto the high-speed facility and transfer waiting time to the ramp. Generally such a procedure results in reduced total travel time.

If most ramps are metered, the flow conditions on the expressway can be predetermined. Leaving aside unsolved problems of equity in the metering process, one could decide that buses should have priority in the ramp queues.[b] This would require that some special attention be given to geometric design, but this is not an unsolvable problem. It would also be possible to integrate the design of transfer facilities into the design of the entire highway. The only prerequisite for proper functioning of such a system is the full control of all ramps by means of ramp metering. If the high-speed facility is ever allowed to break down, the advantage given to buses would be lost.

Other service-improving possibilities lie in the area of improving bus loading and unloading in an effort to decrease travel times or to improve the traveler's comfort and convenience. Increasing loading and unloading rates could be accomplished in several ways. The most appealing is the design of a "street level" bus. A great deal of the time lost in entering and leaving buses is spent negotiating the stairs. For the handicapped and the elderly this may represent a major deterrent to the use of the present system. The design of a low level bus would, however, be difficult from an engineering point of view because of tire wells, structural members, etc. A platform level bus would by contrast require loading and unloading platforms for normal use, which would only be useful for line-haul operations.

A mixed system with stairs on one side and platform level loading on the other may make sense for the express bus system described earlier. Local service pickup and delivery could be performed at street level from the right side of the bus while line-haul stops could be accomplished at platform level from the left side. Centralized fare collection at the line-haul stations would make it unnecessary for fare collection to be performed for other than local to local service. The platform design shown in Meyer, Kain, and Wohl,[c] would work equally well for isolated line-haul stations, express bus on separate rights-of-way, or in conjunction with ramp metered expressways.

Other comfort-producing design changes include buses with longer side windows so riders can determine their location. For most systems, good signs and system maps are also greatly needed. New or potential riders need information about where the system goes, what it costs, and system schedules in order to decide whether they can use it or not. Air-conditioning is a valuable amenity in some climates. Attractive design may also be a factor in stimulating and maintaining customer satisfaction. Although we might expect these added features to induce increased transit travel, no quantitative estimates of their affect on ridership are available.

The cost of implementing each of the systems described above, with the exception of express buses on separate rights-of-way, can be accomplished for far less than the subsidy required if the fare were reduced to zero. For the revenues foregone from a comprehensive free transit program, the system can be duplicated in most instances. The additional equipment, drivers, and overhead which this amount of money would purchase could be used either to extend the present system, to increase the schedule frequency, or some of both. Using these

[b]This may readily be justified in view of the number of travelers being delayed. By expediting the bus entry onto the roadway the delay is reduced for a much larger number of persons than if the bus had to wait for automobiles with very few passengers.

[c]J.R. Meyer, J.F. Kain, and M. Wohl, *The Urban Transportation Problem*, Cambridge,

funds to increase schedule frequency at line-haul or feeder stations appears especially desirable in conjunction with improved local bus collection and distribution systems.

Construction of separate ways for exclusive use of buses would be expensive, but not as expensive as the construction of present-day expressways. The construction costs for separate rights-of-way for express buses appears to vary from $100,000 to $1 million per mile. The design speed of the busway does not have to be as high as that of an expressway in order to give equivalent service, since traffic volumes on this busway would probably be relatively low. Thus, the busway could have more curves or other speed changes than a typical expressway. In some cities it might be practical to consider separate bus streets, particularly in the central areas. Terminals should be designed to serve local destinations as closely as possible since one of the natural advantages of public systems is the freedom from having to park.

Massachusetts, Harvard University Press, 1965, p. 382.

4

Effects of Free Transit on Ridership and System Costs in Boston

The subsidy required to finance a program of free transit consists in: (1) the cost of operating and maintaining the present service, plus (2) the costs of accommodating the increase in ridership generated by the elimination of fares, minus (3) any savings produced by the elimination of fare collection. The first item is the amount that would be required to subsidize a free transit program if no additions to capacity were required and if the savings from the elimination of fares were small. To establish some measure of the additional costs that would be required to meet the increase in ridership, we made a detailed, line-by-line examination of the Boston system. These findings are presented in this chapter. In Chapter 5 we use this estimate to draw inferences about the required cost increases that would be needed for the nation as a whole. The available data do not permit direct estimates of the additional service that would be required for transit on a nationwide basis. This chapter also presents an estimate of the cost savings in Boston from eliminating fare collection. These data will also be used in Chapter 5 in estimating the subsidy requirements for the nation as a whole.

Increased Ridership

Estimating the cost of accommodating the increased ridership generated by the zero fare is a complicated, iterative process. First, we need an estimate of the increase in transit ridership. This is by no means an unambiguous concept. Ideally, we would like to estimate the increase in ridership resulting only from the decrease in fare and the subsequent changes in travel time brought about by the elimination of fare collection. All other service levels should be held constant in order to separate the effects of the zero fare from the effects of changes in service.

In Chapter 3 we concluded that travel times are likely to remain roughly constant in response to the elimination of the fare as long as capacity is not strained. However, such aspects of service as the probability of obtaining a seat, comfort, room for packages, etc. are likely to deteriorate as load factors increase, even though capacity is not filled and trip times remain roughly constant. To account for these changes in service it is desirable to hold load factors constant. However, adding capacity to hold load factors constant reduces headways, which in turn reduces waiting time, which is an important improvement in service. Thus, it does not seem possible to hold service levels constant and measure only the increase in ridership resulting from the elimination of fares. To obtain the best approximation of the ideal measure of ridership response,we held load factors constant except where seats would be available for all riders even with the increase in ridership. Then we measured separately: (1) the increase in demand resulting from the zero fare together with the time savings directly attributable to the elimination of fares; and (2) the increase in demand resulting from shorter headways. This at least provides a rough measure of the increase in ridership attributable to service changes as opposed to the elimination of fares.

This general procedure was followed: An initial estimate was made of the change in transit trips that would result from eliminating the fare. In these estimates we assumed that the elimination of fares would not reduce the boarding time per passenger on rapid transit. For buses, we assumed a decrease in loading times per passenger of one second. The resulting increase in demand was computed by line and by hour of the day. Then the resulting trip volumes were examined to determine when and where seats would not be available for all riders, necessitating additional vehicles so that pre-existing load factors could be approximately maintained (given the discontinuities arising from the need to add entire vehicles and complete shifts). The effect of introducing the required new capacity on headways and waiting times was then estimated. We assumed the decrease in waiting time was one-half the reduction in the headway. Then a second estimate was made of ridership. This time both the elimination of fares and the changes in waiting times were taken into account. The new travel volumes were compared to capacities to see if still more vehicles were needed. In the few cases where they were, they were added and the accompanying adjustments to demand were made until the process converged.

As discussed in Chapter 2, it was necessary to extrapolate the demand functions so that the results of a zero fare could be estimated. The elasticities of the demand functions taken at the means were used to compute these changes in demand.

The elasticities computed at the means were also used to eliminate the effects on demand of changes in the various service variables. This was done to give comparable treatment to all system performance variables in the model. As discussed earlier, only the work and shopping trip equations were used; the equations for shopping trips, which comprise roughly one-third of home-based nonwork trips, were assumed to represent all nonwork trips.

In determining the fare elasticity for work trips, it is necessary to take account of combination trips, those involving more than one transit mode, since the access cost variable includes the feeder bus fare. Based on discussions with MBTA officials as well as a hand analysis of a small sample of representative lines from the Boston Regional Planning Project postcard survey, we assumed that three-fourths of transit trips are combination trips. As noted in Chapter 2, this assumption yields a fare elasticity for work trips of -.17 and for shopping trips of -.323.

To take account of the time savings of one second per passenger from the elimination of fare collection, we assumed an average of sixty passengers per one-way bus trip in the peak hours, or one minute saved per trip. We assumed the same savings in off-peak travel, although actually the somewhat lower load factors would reduce the time savings. This short-cut inflates the ridership increases slightly, but does not affect the cost estimates, because there are only a few instances where additional capacity is needed in the off-peak. The ridership figures are inflated only slightly because the percentage savings in travel time are small and the time elasticities are low.

Estimation of the effect on ridership of reductions in bus loading times is complicated by the fact that feeder bus travel times are included in the access time variables in the demand model, but when bus is the principal mode, the loading time is included in the line-haul time variable. For shopping trips this distinction is not a complicating factor because these two components of travel time were aggregated into one variable. For work trips, however, the two components of transit travel time are separate and have different elasticities, which, fortunately, are not widely different, being -0.7 and -0.4 for access and line-haul times respectively. We used an elasticity of -0.6, the same elasticity as for shopping trips and roughly the weighted average of the two work-trip demand elasticities, assuming that three-fourths of bus trips are feeder bus trips. In any event, the time savings from reduction of bus loading times do not greatly add to ridership. For example, the average one-way transit access time in Boston is about twenty-four minutes (see Table A-9).[a] A one-minute reduction (a reduction of 1/24) multiplied by an elasticity of -0.6 results in an increase in transit trips of (-1/24) $\times$ (-0.6) = 0.025, or 2.5 percent.

The fare and travel time elasticities were applied by hour of day to a tabulation of the 1963 O&D survey giving the directional work trips distributed by hour of arrival.[b] The tabulation also gives, by hour of day, the percentage that work trips comprise of total transit trips. We assumed that all trips in the 5:00 to 9:00 A.M. period are work trips, thus ascribing the work fare elasticity to morning school trips, for which we have no demand model.

These computations resulted in an average percentage increase in transit trips for each hour of the day. The average is computed as the percentage increase in work trips weighted by the fraction of work trips, plus the percentage increase in nonwork trips weighted by the fraction of nonwork trips. The percentage increases ranged from about 20 percent in the morning peak, when it was assumed that all trips were work trips, to about 34 percent in the mid-day (1:00

[a]For feeder bus service, for example, this includes walking to and from the bus stop, transfer and waiting time, as well as the feeder bus line-haul time.

[b]The tabulation (Tab IX) was prepared by Alan M. Voorhees and Associates using the Wilbur Smith and Associates 1963 Origin and Destination Survey.

to 3:00 P.M.), when almost 90 percent of transit trips are nonwork trips. The overall increase in transit ridership was about 28 percent.

These hour-of-day percentage increases were then applied to 1967 MBTA cordon count data to estimate the increase in ridership by line. These estimated increases were used to make a first approximation estimate of new equipment requirements. The reductions in headways resulting from the additional equipment were then calculated and it was assumed that the reduction in waiting time was half the reduction in the headway. The access time elasticities of -0.7 and -0.6 for work and shopping trips respectively were applied to the percentage decreases in access times resulting from the additional equipment to estimate the additional ridership stimulated by the reduction in headways. These computations added four percentage points to the previous increase in ridership, resulting in a total increase from both the elimination of fares and the addition of new capacity of about 32 percent.

Costs of Added Service

In determining new capacity requirements, it was assumed that where standees are presently scheduled, the same loading standard would be adhered to in adjusting the service. Thus the percentage variations in vehicle loading (ranging from thirty-five passengers per bus in the peak hour on some lines to ninety on others) was maintained.[c] In nonrush hours, no change in service was provided unless standees resulted. Based on these assumptions, we estimated that 137 additional buses and sixty subway cars would be needed.

Mileage added was computed by tallying the number of new trips for each bus, streetcar, and rapid transit line and multiplying by the MBTA official round-trip mileage. This resulted in an estimate of additional annual mileage of 3.5 million miles for bus service, 0.3 million for streetcar, and 2.6 million for subway.

The number of operators (bus drivers, motormen, etc.) required was derived from peak period added vehicle requirements. The MBTA is bound by contract to limit swing shifts over eleven hours in spread to 30 percent of all runs (other large systems are being similarly constrained; at present on the subway lines in New York, no swing shifts are allowed by contract.) Thus, if twenty morning and twenty-four afternoon peak period additional vehicles were required at a given garage, ten swing shifts could handle ten of the morning and ten of the afternoon vehicles; another twenty-four would be needed for the remaining trips. Some of these twenty-four would be usable for nonpeak increases in service to provide for the projected needs; the remainder would be paid eight

[c]While this procedure is inconsistent with the simplifying assumption of sixty passengers per bus used to calculate the savings in loading time per passenger trip, the assumption helps substantially in computing the increase in ridership without significantly affecting the results.

hours for a few hours' work. The estimated increase in operators was 221 regular and ninety-seven swing shifts.[d]

The costs of the added vehicles, mileage, and operators were estimated as follows:

Vehicles

Buses were assumed to cost $34,000 each (air-conditioned). We assumed a twelve-year life, no scrap value, and a 6 percent interest rate to annualize the costs of these vehicles.[e] This resulted in an estimated annual cost of $0.5 million.

$$(137 \text{ buses}) \times (\$34,000 \text{ per bus}) \times$$
$$(.11928 \text{ capital recovery factor for 12 years at 6\%})$$
$$\text{equals } \$555,000 \text{ per year.}$$

Subway cars were estimated to cost $135,000 per vehicle, to have an expected life of thirty years and no scrap value.[f] This yields an annual cost figure of $0.6 million.

$$(60 \text{ vehicles}) \times (\$135,000 \text{ per vehicle}) \times$$
$$(.07265 \text{ capital recovery factor for 30 years at 6\%})$$
$$\text{equals } \$588,000 \text{ per year.}$$

Mileage

Vehicle operating costs were estimated to be $.41 per mile for bus, $.66 for subway and $.75 for streetcar. These figures were based on the thirteen-month MBTA figures ended September 30, 1967. They yield an annual estimate of $3.3 million.

---

[d]It was found in making the capacity estimates that the Watertown car line would have to be converted to bus operation in order to free sufficient vehicles for increases in service on the other streetcar lines. The storage facilities at Galen Street were thus assumed to be converted to bus storage, and used for other lines now based at Somerville Garage as well, to ease the overload there. A new bus garage would have to be opened on MBTA land at either Fields Corner, Ashmont, or Mattapan to accommodate the additional vehicles required on lines now based at the Albany, Bartlett, and Arborway Garages. The costs of these garages or of increased rapid transit storage facilities were not computed. This, of course, lowers the estimate of the annual cost increase, but on an annualized basis these fixed facilities would probably not add a great deal to the cost estimates.

[e]These figures are discussed in more detail in Chapter 5.

[f]See the discussion in Chapter 5. Also, the cost of the last MBTA order was $110,000 per car, delivered in 1963. The current NYCTA R-38 contract deliveries are $112,500 per car plus $20,000 (approximately) for airconditioning.

$$(\$.41) \times (3.5 \text{ million miles}) = \$1.4 \text{ million}$$

$$(\$.66) \times (2.6 \text{ million miles}) = \$1.7 \text{ million}$$

$$(\$.75) \times (0.3 \text{ million miles}) = \underline{\$0.2} \text{ million}$$

$$\$3.3 \text{ million}$$

Operators

Operators on the MBTA system are now paid $5.25 per hour, including all fringes and benefits (but not swing spread overtime for runs of over eleven hours). This results in daily figures of $42 for eleven-hour swing runs. The daily figures were multiplied by 300 days for regular shifts and by 250 for swing shifts to reach an annual figure. This assumes that the net effect of uncalculated increases in service on weekends plus reserve is a sixth weekday. The annual increase in operator cost based on these figures is $4 million.

$$(\$42) \times (300) \times (221) = \$2.8 \text{ million}$$

$$(\$49) \times (250) \times (\ 97) = \underline{\$1.2} \text{ million}$$

$$\$4.0 \text{ million}$$

Summary of Cost Increase

Summing these annual cost figures yields a total of $8.4 million.

Vehicles	Annual Cost
Bus	$0.5 million
Subway	$0.6 million
Mileage	$3.3 million
Operators	$4.0 million
Total	$8.4 million

Using this Boston estimate of the added costs required to accommodate the increased ridership to draw inferences about the added costs for the nation as a whole requires normalizing the Boston figure. This is best done by determining the percentage increase in current Boston costs required to service the added riders. To do this we need an estimate of current MBTA operating and capital costs. We used recent MBTA cost figures for this purpose, recognizing that these figures undoubtedly significantly understate capital costs because accounting depreciation figures do not reflect current replacement costs. Nevertheless, the accounting figures are adequate, as will be seen more clearly in Chapter 5, for the gross estimates needed for the nation as a whole.

MBTA operating costs for the thirteen months ending September 30, 1967, were $65.3 million. Fixed charges comprising interest, depreciation, and rentals were $11 million, making total costs for the thirteen-month period $76.3 million. Reduced to a twelve-month figure, this is $70.4 million. The $8.4 million per year cost of added capacity represents about 12 percent of this twelve-month cost.

Savings from the Elimination of Fare Collection

The annual costs of fare collection supplied by MBTA were as follows:

Station Receivers (collectors in bus garages)	$ .375 million
Money Collection Room at HQ	$ .715 million
Auditing of Day Cards at HQ	$ .115 million
Collectors (station booth agents)	$1.975 million
Fare Box & Turnstile Maintenance	$ .175 million
Gatemen	$ .100 million
	$3.455 million

In Boston a starter or porter is on duty at most subway stations all day long. Thus, if fares were eliminated, in principle collectors could be eliminated since the starters or porters would be available to fulfill the information and protection functions now provided in part by the collectors. Of course, institutional restraints might delay or prevent the elimination of collectors.

Summary of Costs

Totaling the three components of cost gives a lower limit estimate of the public funds required to support free transit in Boston, because the current costs, using accounting capital charges based on original cost, probably understate the cost of replacement. The sum is about $75.3 million.

Current Costs	$70.4 million
Cost of Added Capacity	$ 8.4 million
Cost of Fare Collection	$-3.5 million
	$75.3 million

5

Public Funds Required for Nationwide Free Transit Service

As mentioned in the previous chapter there are three aspects to computing the public funds required to finance a program of free transit: (1) the cost of the present service; (2) the cost of additional capacity required to serve the increase in ridership; and (3) any savings from the elimination of fare collection.

Reasonably good estimates of the nationwide costs of operating and maintaining the present service can be made from available published data. These cost estimates are given in the first section of this chapter. However, data are not available to make nationwide estimates of the additional service needed to accommodate the increased ridership. Rough estimates based on our Boston study are used for this purpose. Following this is a discussion of the likely savings in collection costs from eliminating the fare.

Cost of Maintaining the Present Service

Estimates of the costs of subsidizing free, or reduced fare, public transportation operations can be based either on the loss of revenue or on the total costs.[a] It does not seem appropriate to use foregone revenue as an estimate of the subsidy cost when some transit systems are already substantially subsidized, and others are self-sustaining or even profitable while paying their full cost. The amount of revenue collected is, to some extent, dependent on fare policies of individual operating authorities and hence does not represent a uniform basis for estimating the subsidy costs of a system. Total costs may also vary among individual companies due to such variables as operating policies, union scales, and work rules, but in some meaningful sense total costs do represent the allocation of resources to public transportation.

The following sections describe the estimates of nationwide transit system costs and the methodology by which they were calculated. For purposes of analysis it is desirable to have some breakdown of the costs into broad components which may vary independently under alternative operating or subsidy policies. The cost estimates presented here for existing systems separate labor, materials, capital costs of vehicles, capital costs of other fixed facilities, and taxes. It should be emphasized that it is not the purpose of this section to provide a detailed company-by-company cost analysis for potential use in determining the distribution of individual subsidies, but rather to provide an aggregate estimate of total costs. Although crude, these analyses are useful in defining the general magnitude of the costs that may be involved for subsidizing free transit systems on a nationwide basis.

[a]The American Transit Association estimates total annual transit operating revenue for 1966 at $1.479 billion.

Data Sources

The primary sources for data on transit costs are the various publications of the American Transit Association (ATA), which makes a continuing study of transit operations in the United States. The ATA annually receives detailed financial and operational data for individual transit companies, which are tabulated and reported in its *Transit Operating Reports.* These reports consist in four volumes: system-wide totals, motor bus operations, railway operations, and trolley coach operations.

According to the 1967 edition of the ATA's *Transit Fact Book,* that contains 1966 summary data on the transit industry, there were over 1,100 operating transit companies in the United States at the close of 1966. ATA claims to receive financial and statistical reports from some 85 percent of the transit industry (presumably measured by volume, rather than number of companies). The system-wide totals volume of the *Transit Operating Reports* gives data for 128 U. S. companies, which is slightly over 10 percent of the number of operating companies. However, when measured on the basis of either revenue or operating costs, the 128 reporting companies account for over 75 percent of the reported national totals.

The ATA informs us that the *Fact Book* data are not simple extrapolations of the annual *Transit Operating Reports* data but are built on a periodic benchmark study (last made about ten years ago) in which detailed analyses are made of reported data on individual companies and other information in order to produce national aggregate estimates. The annual updates to the *Fact Book* are made on the basis of year-to-year changes in selected indicators for the reporting companies. It was acknowledged by ATA personnel that the relationships between the *Transit Operating Reports* data and national totals were subject to change over time, and that this problem became increasingly serious as time passed since the last benchmark study.

Because the *Transit Operating Reports* are current, they would be a very desirable source to estimate nationwide costs. Unfortunately, the data in this source introduce other significant problems, including, to mention only a few, the nonreporting of some data by individual companies (some of them large), particularly passenger statistics; differences in accounting and reporting practices among companies; differences in the nature of basic operations (*e.g.*, city versus suburban versus intercity, and all combinations of these); and differences in capital costs and tax situations, especially between private and public operations.

Despite all these deficiencies, the ATA data represent the most complete and timely set of transit operating data available from a single source. The consistency of these data, while less than perfect, seems to be far greater than can be readily achieved from any other available source. Further, for the order-of-magnitude estimates required for the purposes of this study, the level of precision afforded by the ATA data is probably sufficient, if the nature and limitations of the data are kept in mind in interpreting the quantitative estimates.

Cost Calculations

For the purposes of this study the major cost elements of transit operations are defined as:

1. Labor
2. Materials
3. Depreciation or capital recovery
4. Taxes

Clearly, much finer breakdowns of each of these categories can be made, and indeed more detail does appear in the ATA *Transit Operating Reports* and elsewhere, but for this study, the above breakdown will suffice.

In Table 1 of the *Fact Book*, 1966 aggregate operating expenses are estimated to be $1.424 billion, including depreciation. Taxes are estimated separately as $92 million. In order to overcome differences in company accounting practices, we attempted to make another estimate of transit costs, using the expense categories presented above.

The *Fact Book* lists total payrolls for 1966 of $995 million, and total expenditures for materials of $180 million. These figures are presumably straightforward estimates and no attempt was made to reestimate them. To bring these figures up to 1967 levels, some adjustment is required. Assuming that total labor costs increased about 4 percent between 1966 and 1967, estimated 1967 labor cost is $1,035 million.[b] There was probably no substantial increase in the cost of operating or of maintenance materials.[c]

Because of great variation in depreciation policies and company operating

[b]The Bureau of Labor Statistics in its *Employment and Earnings and Monthly Report on the Labor Force* series, reports an approximate 4½ percent increase from 1966 to 1967 in average weekly earnings of production workers in SIC 411 — Local and Suburban Transportation. The figure is approximate because final 1967 annual figures have not been published as of this writing, although preliminary monthly figures are available.

[c]The January 1968 *Survey of Current Business*, U.S. Department of Commerce, shows wholesale price indices for refined petroleum products of 100.4 in December 1967, as opposed to 100.2 in December 1966 (1957-59 = 100). The motor vehicles and equipment wholesale price index increased from 101.7 to 104.0 in the same period. However, a large component of the change of this latter index results from the impact of safety equipment on the prices of new vehicles, especially passenger cars.

practices, independent estimates of annual capital recovery costs are required to assure consistent treatment of all companies.

For all capital recovery cost calculations, an annual discount rate of 6 percent was assumed. Arguments can be made for using a lower rate, such as the rate municipalities might pay for tax-exempt bond financing, or for a higher rate, such as the opportunity costs of higher yield commercial investments. Since, for the purpose of this study, we are interested in the total expenditures that would be required to operate the transit systems, the opportunity cost concept, which is not a reflection of cash expenditures, may not be entirely appropriate. Furthermore, the tax-exempt municipal bond rate is, in effect, an artificially low one simply because part of the rate is paid by the federal government in the form of foregone tax revenue. Therefore, it seems appropriate to use rates that might be required for a government guaranteed bond without tax exemption, *i.e.*, the yield of federal government securities, and a rate of 6 percent was selected for the analysis. While this is believed to be a reasonable rate, the same methodology would apply if other rates were used to calculate the costs.

In the following discussion we first estimate the annual capital costs for rolling stock, and then estimate the costs of supporting facilities.

Rolling Stock

Subway and Elevated. The *Fact Book* reports a 1966 fleet of 9,273 vehicles. Dividing gross investment for rapid transit ($3.2 billion) by the number of subway and elevated vehicles in the fleet[d] yields an average investment in transit facilities (cars plus supporting facilities) of over $340,000 per car. There is substantial variation in the costs of rapid transit cars due to differences in system and vehicle design in various cities, but a survey yielded a typical current cost per car of $135,000. The gross investment per car for rapid transit is over 2.5 times the current replacement value of a car, which illustrates the large investment needed for supporting facilities.

Calculating the current replacement cost of subway and elevated rolling stock, assuming a thirty-year life, no scrap value, and 6 percent interest, we have:[e]

Annual capital cost for rapid transit cars =
(9,273 vehicles) X ($135,000 per vehicle) X
(.07265 capital recovery factor for 30 years
at 6%),

yielding a capital cost of $90 million per year for the nationwide system.

Bus. We assumed that the bus fleet will include not only the vehicles required to service routes presently operated with buses, but also those required to service routes presently operated with surface rail (streetcar) and trolley bus, as these

---

[d]The fleet has been approximately the same in size since 1950, and is only about 15 percent smaller than the peak fleet of 11,000 vehicles in 1940.

[e]The assumption regarding the life of the vehicles is based on J. R Meyer, *et. al., op. cit.*, p. 178. The assumption of no scrap value is based on discussions with transit officials.

latter two vehicles are no longer in production and their routes are generally being converted to bus service as equipment is retired. The 1966 fleet consisted of:

50,130 motor buses
1,407 surface rail cars
1,326 trolley coaches

52,863 total vehicles

The *Transit Fact Book* lists a gross investment of $986 million for motor bus, and $1.2 billion if surface rail and trolley coach are added. In the latter two cases, however, gross investment includes substantial investments in rails, overhead wires, and, in some cases, special rights-of-way and power plants. Using only the motor bus data, we have an average investment of $986 million divided by 50,130 vehicles, or slightly less than $20,000 per vehicle. This investment figure includes not only buses but presumably also yards and shops for bus storage and maintenance.

Bus fleet capital costs were calculated at current cost levels as with rail transit vehicles. The current cost of a bus was assumed to be $34,000.[c] Assuming a twelve-year life, no scrap value, and a 6 percent interest rate, the fleet of 52,863 vehicles would have an annual capital cost of $214.4 million, derived as follows:[g]

(52,863 vehicles) $\times$ ($34,000 per vehicle) $\times$
(.11928 capital recovery factor for 12 years at 6 %).

Supporting Facilities

Calculating the capital cost for fixed facilities is a much more difficult task than for rolling stock, for several reasons. First, capital costs for fixed facilities are heavily influenced by physical characteristics of the area, including density of population, and geography. Second, we do not have the advantage of having an active market of buyers and sellers of these facilities, as we have for rolling stock, and thus cannot obtain average prices for new facilities. Third, part of

[f] This figure is for a standard large urban bus with airconditioning and appears to be typical in light of responses to our own inquiries and data gathered by the ATA in 1967.

[g] Current lives of buses used for accounting purposes vary from company to company, but are generally slightly longer than twelve years. While buses may be economically capable of serving passengers for a longer period of time, one transit official stated that after a while they become "aesthetically obsolete" and passengers dislike riding the very old equipment. The twelve-year life is assumed in J.R. Meyer, *et. al., Ibid.* According to transit industry officials, retired buses have very little, if any, scrap value. For the

purposes of these calculations it was assumed that any scrap value would be insignificant and was therefore ignored.

gross investment may include real estate, which may have significantly more value than its original cost and in most cases does not depreciate physically.

Subway and Elevated. Although factors are available to estimate the capital costs of the fixed facilities necessary in conjunction with a rapid transit system, they require detailed engineering estimates of operating parameters for which we have no data.[h]

By using the gross investment in rapid transit systems and assumptions about the fleet, we can calculate what is most probably a minimum value of the gross investment in fixed facilities. This was done by assuming that the entire fleet of rolling stock has the value of new equipment, and subtracting this total from the gross investment at book value to obtain an estimate of the investment in fixed rapid transit facilities.[i] Estimated gross book value of investment in rapid transit = $3.17 billion minus:

> Value of rolling stock (at replacement value)
> $135,000 per vehicle $\times$ 9,273 vehicles = $1.25 billion

equals:

> Estimated minimum value of fixed
>   rapid transit investment $1.92 billion

Assuming a fifty-year life, no scrap value and 6 percent interest, we have

Annual capital costs for rapid transit system fixed facilities =
($1.92 billion) $\times$ (.06344 capital recovery factor 50 years at 6 %
or
$122 million per year capital cost.[j]

Buses. Since the gross investment in the bus system is less than the product of the number of buses times the current cost per bus, we cannot calculate the fixed facilities costs for these systems by subtracting the rolling stock cost from

[h]J.R. Meyer, *et. al., op. cit.,* pp. 371 *ff.*

[i]The reasons this procedure is believed to result in a minimum estimate are that current values of rapid transit vehicles are probably far in excess of the original costs used in calculating the gross investment. Moreover, the book values of way and structures, stations, yards and shops are probably substantially less than their current replacement costs. Assuming a lower cost per car or a higher value for the associated fixed investment will yield a higher annual capital cost.

[j]If an infinite life were assumed, which is reasonable for much of this investment (especially the real estate) if proper maintenance is provided, there is no significant difference in capital cost.

the gross investment (as was done for rapid transit). Meyer, Kain, and Wohl give investment in yards and shops per bus as $4,500 and a life of forty years.[k] Using their data, and assuming no scrap value, we have

Annual capital costs for bus system fixed facilities = (52,863 vehicles) X ($4,500 invested in yards and shops per vehicle) X (.06646 capital recovery factor for 40 years at 6 %).

yielding a capital cost of $15.8 million per year.[l]

Taxes

The 1966 taxes paid by transit systems from the 1967 *Transit Fact Book* (Table No. 2), were as follows:

	Amount ($ Millions)	Percent of Total
Federal Taxes (Total)	58.7	64
Income Taxes ($14.9 million)		16
Other Federal Taxes ($43.9 million)		48
State, County and Local Taxes	33.1	36
Total Taxes	91.8	100

Ideally, we would like to have a measure of the costs of additional public services required in conjunction with providing transit services. Some costs are properly attributed to the transit operation. If there were no existing subsidies to transit systems or tax concessions made to them, taxes paid might be used to provide a reasonable measure of these costs, but such is not the case. Some systems are subsidized, *e.g.*, some tax revenues are returned to the transit companies to offset costs. To the extent that this occurs, some degree of double counting occurs when the total of all taxes is added to the costs. On the other hand, to the extent tax concessions are made, the aggregate of tax payments made by the transit companies may fall short of the cost of the additional public services required to support the transit system. There is no reason to assume that these effects are offsetting; in fact, it seems reasonable to assume that the taxes paid underestimate the costs of the additional public services and, at least, can provide a conservative estimate of these costs. For this reason the $92 million tax figure has been included in our cost estimate.

[k] *op. cit.*, p. 383.

[l] As in the rapid transit case, if we assume an infinite life, which would be the case if all the investment were land, the difference in annual capital charges would be insignificant.

The federal income tax component of tax costs suggests another problem which cannot be dismissed lightly. While most of the transit operations in the major metropolitan areas are now public and not run for profit, there is still a significant number of private transit firms whose owners seek a fair return on their investment. The federal income tax figure itself can be used to give a minimum estimate of the magnitude of these profits. The table above shows federal income taxes in 1966 of $14.9 million. If we assume that all this tax arose from corporate profits taxed at the 48 percent maximum federal rate, this would imply a profit of $33 million. In fact, of course, all the profit is not taxed at the 48 percent rate, and the true taxable profit is undoubtedly somewhat larger. Further, some account should be taken off the private firms which, for some reason, did not make a profit. In any subsidy situation, all the private firms will demand a fair return for their investment, and this will have to be provided, unless all private transit firms are to be acquired by public authorities. This latter step would, of course, involve other significant costs, at least in the short run. The 6 percent return that has been assumed for purposes of capital equipment financing cannot be assumed to provide a sufficient return for the investors of a completely private operation, since the total capitalization of a transit operation may be significantly in excess of its capital equipment, and presumably this additional capital is also entitled to a fair rate of return. We have not estimated the additional amount that would be required to provide a fair return on this capital; hence, the costs may be somewhat understated.

To summarize the above calculations, we have annual costs of:

Labor	$1,035 million
Materials	180 million
Rolling Stock — Bus	214 million
Rolling Stock — Rapid Transit	91 million
Fixed Investment — Bus	16 million
Fixed Investment — Rapid Transit	122 million
Taxes	92 million
	$1,750 million

The figure of $1,750 million is our estimate of the current annual cost of operating and maintaining the present service on the nation's transit systems.

Cost of Accommodating Additional Riders

Additional costs would be incurred to provide the same level of service as now prevails for the larger number of riders which would be stimulated by the free fare. Because of differences in coverage of the various transit operators, the ATA data do not provide useable figures on load factors for determining the increases in service that would be required to accommodate the additional traffic. Thus, we estimated the increased costs that would be needed for Boston and used this estimate to generalize about the nation as a whole. Obviously, this approach gives at best only a rough approximation, but, as will be seen below, the results it yields are reasonable.

In Boston the annualized cost of the added capacity needed to hold load factors roughly constant amounted to about 12 percent of current costs. This is very likely an overestimate of the percentage increase in costs because the capital costs of the additional service are based on current equipment replacement costs, whereas the accounting fixed charges are based on original costs. However, the major portion of both the cost of additional capacity and the current costs is made up of labor and mileage costs rather than fixed charges. The estimates of operating expenses to accommodate the additions to capacity are directly comparable to current expenses because they are based on the same wage rates, prices of materials, and so forth.

A second possible objection to using Boston cost figures to generalize about the nationwide costs is that Boston is generally conceded to be a very high cost operation. However, this difficulty is largely overcome by putting the costs of additional capacity on a percentage basis.

If we apply the 12 percent figure to the estimate of $1.75 billion, the current annual cost of maintaining the present capacity for the nation as a whole, we obtain an estimate of $0.21 billion as the additional annual cost required to accommodate the increased ridership. The sum of the two is $1.96 billion, or say $2 billion in round numbers.

It can very easily be seen that the figure of $2 billion is not especially sensitive to the rough method of estimating the cost of additional service. If a gross correction is made in the 12 percent figure to account for the underestimate of replacement costs in the Boston accounting figures, the results are changed only slightly. For example, assume the actual cost figures in Boston are as much as 50 percent higher than the reported figures. This would lower the 12 percent figure to 8 percent, yielding an estimate of $0.14 billion as the cost of additional capacity which, when added to the figure of $1.75 billion, gives a total cost figure of $1.89 billion. This is only slightly below the estimate of $1.96 billion. On the other hand, assume the cost of added capacity is proportional to the increase in ridership. The estimated increase in ridership for Boston is 32 percent, including the riders generated by the reduction in headways. Applying this percentage to the estimate of $1.75 billion yields an estimate of $0.56 billion as the cost of added capacity. The sum of the two cost figures is $2.31 billion, an amount somewhat above the earlier estimate, but probably not enough above to make much difference for planning purposes.

Savings from Elimination of Fare Collection

For Boston, we estimated that the elimination of the costs associated with fare collection would reduce system costs by about $3.5 million dollars, about 5 percent of current system costs. About $2 million of this amount, however, is the cost of station booth agents at subway stations and these savings would only be achieved by systems which have rapid transit service. There are five of these systems at present, Boston, New York, Philadelphia, Cleveland, and Chicago, with a sixth system, in San Francisco, under construction. Even for these few cities, the cost of subway collectors would only be saved fully if other personnel were available to provide the information and protection functions also furnished by collectors. In Boston there are starters or porters on duty all day at most stations to provide this service, but this is not the case for all subway systems, *e.g.* New York. Where other personnel are not already on duty to provide information and protection, collectors would have to be replaced by others, who might be equally or more costly (police, for example). For this reason, the New York City Transit Authority recently compiled an estimate of the savings from eliminating fare collection and concluded that they would be negligible and indeed costs might even increase.

From the foregoing discussion, it appears that the cost savings from the elimination of fare collection probably range from zero to something less than 5 percent of current costs and are small enough to be regarded as negligible for the nation as a whole. For example, if we assumed that they were 1 to 2 percent of current costs, they would not materially affect our earlier rough estimate of $2 billion. Therefore, it seems reasonable to conclude that the public expenditure required to support a nationwide system of free transit is on the general order of $2 billion per year.

Efficiency of Free Transit in Meeting Policy Objectives

If the goals of public policy were clearly stated, an evaluation of the alternatives available to achieve those goals would be relatively simple. In fact, however, there are few goals in a democratic society on which all persons agree. Indeed, the goals of public policy are often subject to frequent change, are sometimes mutually inconsistent, and are almost always poorly defined. This creates an important problem in evaluating free transit or any other program of public investment in transportation services because there is no agreed objective by which alternatives can be measured. There is no "ideal" transportation system apart from the ends which are served, and perhaps the most important and difficult task is to determine those ends for which intervention in the transportation market is a reasonable and efficient means.

In this chapter of the report, we first discuss a number of possible justifications for public subsidy of mass transit operations in general, without focusing on free transit subsidies in particular. Following this we examine the effectiveness of free transit in meeting a number of specified objectives. In each case alternative means of promoting the same goals are examined so that an evaluation of the relative efficiency of free transit in meeting these objectives can be made.

Possible Justifications for Use of Mass Transit Subsidies

Management Assistance

One possible rationale for public transit subsidy is to provide management aid to transit systems, that is, to effectuate better transit planning, to improve the use of old technologies and develop new ones, and to enact more enlightened pricing and marketing schemes.

Generally speaking, mass transit management has not exhibited an outstanding record.[a] It has been criticized for ineffectiveness in scheduling and resistance to new ideas in marketing of transit services. Extensive recruiting of top management personnel from line positions has hampered entry of potential transit managers with relevant experience in other fields. Further, resistance in the past of both labor unions and local public officials has often prevented transit management from implementing worthwhile innovations.

However, the market for transit service faces stiff competition from the auto, and hence presents a difficult challenge even for the most proficient management. The need for management assistance is widely recognized. Public grants

[a]For a detailed discussion of transit management records and problems, see Lewis M. Schneider, *Marketing Urban Mass Transit: A Comparative Study of Management Strategies,* Graduate School of Business Administration, Harvard University, 1965.

might be in order not only because innovation presents risks, but because what can be learned is often useful beyond the market of any single transit operation. In general, long-run prospects of nonauto systems might be technologically and economically feasible, but these involve major uncertainties and unknowns. The limitations of rail transit as it presently exists to serve medium to high density corridors must be realized; nevertheless, the difficulties involved in relying solely on private automobiles suggest an important role for some form of transit service. Insufficient effort has been expended in a serious search for transit alternatives (such as mixed mode systems using buses with special rights-of-way to urban highways). Such a program will probably require substantial public financial support since any given development may not provide sufficient payoff to attract private firms in any one city and since such attempts at innovation may be accompanied by considerable risk.

Subsidy can also provide temporary relief so that needed transit services are not abandoned while such research continued. Systems which will be economically efficient over the long run will surely require most or all of present capital and management facilities.

Relief of Central City Tax Burdens

A mass transit subsidy program could have significant tax redistribution effects, transferring tax funds from rural and suburban communities to central cities. Transit subsidies might provide an acceptable program for putting federal funds into central cities, thereby alleviating some of their financial difficulties.

Although a comprehensive examination of metropolitan finances is not possible here, Pidot's study provides some perspective on the general problem.[b] In examining the expenditures and revenues of the eighty largest Standard Metropolitan Statistical Areas (SMSA's) in 1957, he finds that in thirty-nine SMSA's with a large share of their population living in suburbs, government expenditures were about 25 percent higher in the central city on a per capita basis or as a percent of total income. In the central city per capita outlays were two to three times higher for police and fire protection, welfare, sanitation, and parks and recreation. On the other hand, outlays for school construction and maintenance, highway upkeep, and hospital building were higher per capita in the suburbs. On the revenue side, the central city's sources of revenue reflect more alternatives than the property tax, but the central city itself has less of an economic base on which to impose these taxes. The central cities are already very reliant on state and federal aid, and this dependence is likely to increase.

[b]George B. Pidot, *The Public Finances of local Gvoernment in the Metropolitan United States,* Ph.D. Thesis, Department of Economics, Harvard University, July 1965, p. 238.

To considerations of central city fiscal difficulties must be added the history and prospect of state government action. In many states, reapportionment has not sufficiently altered the legislatures' long-standing rural bias. State highway department allocations of funds also have an entrenched rural bias which will be difficult to alter in the short run. Therefore, dependence on the states for relief of core city fiscal problems is questionable for the near future.

It is of course a subjective judgment as to whether the fiscal problems of central cities merit relief and, if they do, how best to provide it. Many feel that some transfer to urban areas is in order, but the methods to be employed are by no means clear. A Brookings study is pessimistic about federal allocations through the states.[c] Federal programs which allocate funds directly to urban areas are perhaps more appropriate, and subsidy to transit is one form which such allocations might take.

It is not clear, however, that a transit subsidy will provide the most productive use of funds for alleviating the cities' financial problems. Not all transit systems are municipally owned, for one thing. Of those which are, not all are deficit operations. Transit revenues for all transit systems taken as a whole are about equal to transit costs (however, transit costs may be understated insofar as depreciation charges do not provide for capital replacement). Moreover, it is not clear that the service improvements which would be desirable in many communities cannot be self-financing. The very low price elasticity estimated for mass transit operations (-.17 for work trips and -.323 for shopping trips) indicates that revenues could be raised through fare increases, as only a relatively small proportion of riders would be lost as a result of the increased fare. For example, according to the work trip price elasticity estimate of -.17, a 20 percent increase in fares would reduce transit work trips by only about 3.5 percent (other things remaining constant), resulting in about a 16 percent increase in revenue from work trips with no accompanying increase in costs. Of course, the increase in fares would cause some diversion to auto and thereby add to auto congestion, but the cross-elasticity figures indicate that that diversion would be small. For work trips, for example, the cross-elasticity of 0.14 indicates that auto work trips would increase by only 2.8 percent as a result of a 20 percent fare increase.

This suggests that municipally owned transit systems need not be a financial drag on the central city. If the low fare elasticities are correct, existing deficits could be corrected by raising fares, and service improvements could also be self-financing. Finally, federal funds to cities might more productively be aimed at other city needs such as welfare, police and fire protection, housing, sanitation, education, and medical facilities. It is true that the availability of federal funds to relieve existing transit deficits would free municipal funds for these other purposes; however, the same amount of funds might be freed by

[c]George F. Break, *Intergovernmental Fiscal Relations in the United States,* The Brookings Institute, January 1967.

raising transit user charges. Then, if the federal money could also be obtained, more total funds would be available for other municipal needs.

Another pressing problem of the central city in most of our large urban areas has resulted from the reduction of taxable property through land-takings for transportation roadways.[d]

To avoid congestion and still maintain an adequate tax base, keeping the automobile out of the central business district has been suggested. Such action, failing to recognize urban society's real transportation needs, might very well restrict the use of the city to those few who have access to good public transit and might be the death knell of the city. The worker who cannot easily use transit or who finds it unpleasant to do so will seek employment elsewhere. As a result employers may find it necessary to pay wages above competitive levels to attract a suitable labor force. This in turn would drive employers to relocate their places of business outside of the central business district. Similarly, establishments such as retail stores, which are dependent on the public to come to them, may lose their customers to the outside areas.

These effects may prevail even when there is very adequate parking at the fringe which is integrated with excellent public transit service to the core area. The inconvenience of changing modes may have such a deleterious effect on trip demand that it more than offsets any benefits that may be attributed to the reduction in congestion. Ample evidence of this possibility is demonstrated by the elasticities of trip demand with respect to out-of-vehicle time shown in Chapter 2.

It is surprising that other solutions have not been more extensively explored and implemented. In particular, much more attention should be given to the use of air rights over the major roads of the central business district; air rights can be used for buildings or for pedestrian malls that would separate people from vehicular traffic, improving the flows through the central business district. Other advantages would also accrue such as keeping the often expensive results of inclement weather from interfering with the flow of traffic in these highly congested areas. It would seem that the use of air rights could make large quantities of land available for transportation without significantly adding to either the cost of building or to any further deterioration of an already inadequate tax base.

[d]The mere reduction in the total land available for building may not in fact destroy taxable property value. Depending on the elasticity of demand for land, the value of remaining land may, in fact, increase by an amount that more than compensates for the lost land. Many factors tend to push in this direction in the case of landtakings for roadways, not the least of which is the increased accessibility to areas as a result of the increased transportation capacity created. Of course, these changes in value may not be reflected if the remaining land is not properly reassessed.

Assistance to Particular Groups

Another broad class of reasons commonly forwarded for mass transit support is based on the aim of redistributing income to particular groups or areas within the city. In this regard, the redistribution motive which may prompt the most support for transit subsidy concerns the central business district. Improved transit service is popularly judged to be a deterrent to decentralization in employment, retail shopping, and residential location.

Meyer, Kain, and Wohl,[e] have presented by far the best and most comprehensive examination of the determinants of land-use changes. They conclude that mass transit facilities are far from the only determinant of changing urban form. The existence of mass facilities does not seem to have had any significant effect on land-use patterns or urban trends in the large. These authors would be the first to admit that the evidence is by no means definitive, and is far short of a full-scale behavioral or feedback model of urban location choices. Nevertheless, evidence should at least be regarded as a serious warning to those who would rely on mass transit to "save" the core city or to reshape land-use patterns.

One can also question the equity of using public funds to subsidize one group of merchants or property owners at the expense of others. The presumption in using public funds to deter decentralized growth is that the dislocations arising from a changing urban form need to be abated somewhat, and that public assistance to transit may lessen the pressures to relocate and hence reduce the rate of decentralization to a level which can be effectuated at a lower social cost. Clearly, this temporary use of public funds to moderate the effects of change frames this motive in a much different light from the case of a long-run commitment to income redistribution to the central business district.

This is not to argue that subsidies are not appropriate, but to suggest that the question must be given thorough consideration before resorting to this solution. Subsidies are often useful for overcoming short-run phenomena. The most efficient allocation of our resources may require a geographic shuffling of activities that will ultimately be induced by the incentives of the marketplace, but in the short run this process may be a very painful one to those adversely affected by the dislocation. Subsidies to mass transit may serve only to distort these natural incentives or to delay appropriate adjustments. On the other hand, subsidy may be a useful tool to alleviate the interim effects of dislocation while adjustment is taking place. Some assurance should be provided, however, that such adjustments will be made and that the subsidy will not permanently serve as an impediment to the natural market forces leading to an improved allocation of resources.

Transit subsidies have also been proposed as a means of benefiting other groups, most commonly, ghetto residents and the aged and handicapped. Implicit in these arguments is the assumption that these groups cannot or should not have to pay the full costs of the service they receive. It is also assumed that transit subsidies are an effective means of relieving the special problems of these persons. Subsidizing the existing transit systems may be a poor means of helping these persons, however, if the present service is not tailored to their needs.

[e]*Op. cit.,* Chapters 2-7.

There is no particular reason to assume that a system designed to move great numbers of people to work at peak hours can provide adequate service for the aged and handicapped, and there is no particular reason to require it to do so. A system requiring the passenger to step up to board a bus, or to climb stairs to reach a subway platform, may be of little or no use for these persons. Separate, special systems might be provided for such special groups, at relatively low cost, without seriously compromising mass transportation needs. Low fare taxi service may be the most appropriate mode for accomodating this rather small fraction of our population. Similarly, for ghetto residents subsidies to the existing service may be of limited benefit if the route structures do not serve their needs.

Reduction of Total Transportation Costs

There are arguments for mass transit subsidy based on a somewhat more favorable assessment of its economic advantages than is evidenced by its current declining market experience, both currently and in the long run. The substance of such arguments is that the financing and pricing of urban highway systems obscure their true costs, and that in certain circumstances transit is actually competitive from a social point of view. The argument has several facets. One is that automobile travel is underpriced when its full social costs are considered (hence, auto usage is subsidized), and therefore public transit should also be subsidized so that consumers' preferences will not be distorted. The facts on this are not clear. It is generally agreed that the construction and maintenance costs of highway facilities are more than covered by highway users, although there may be a cross-subsidy to peak-hour users on the more expensive urban highways and from urban to rural users.[f] These estimates, however, do not cover the external costs to society, such as noise, pollution, dislocation, and aesthetics. Because the valuation of these costs is largely subjective, it is difficult to know whether highway users are subsidized. Nevertheless, if they are, it seems more appropriate to increase highway user charges than to argue for a similar subsidy for transit. Subsidizing both types of service may well lead to a proper allocation of resources between highway and transit, but would result in an improper allocation between transportation facilities and all other goods and services. That is, pricing both highway and transit at less than their full social cost could cause people to consume too much transportation relative to other goods and accordingly lead to over-investment in transportation facilities.

A different but related argument is that transit is a less expensive mode of transportation than automobile and therefore the cost of urban transportation can be lowered by adding transit facilities rather than providing for more cars. Supporters of the argument often measure cost in terms of capacity rather than passengers actually transported. A low cost per transit seat-mile may become an exceedingly high cost per passenger-mile if few passengers are attracted to the facility. The automobile is an expensive mode of transportation, but it offers many features presently unobtainable with any other form of transportation.

[f]See J. R. Meyer, *et. al., op. cit.,* Chapter 4, for a recent summary of the literature.

These include privacy, comfort, freedom from fixed schedules, near door-to-door service, considerable freight carrying capacity on shopping trips, and so forth. These features may fully justify the expense of car travel to travelers. The thrust of these comments is succinctly expressed by Lang and Soberman:

> An evaluation of rail transit relative to either its present or future competitors must thus be set in the context of these costs and service characteristics *as the traveler sees them*. The ultimate test of a transportation system lies not in any technoeconomic indices of efficiency, but in the extent to which it finds acceptance within the total value scheme of the community it serves.[g]

The widespread use of the automobile in spite of its high cost provides evidence that the auto tripmaker places very high values on the qualities of service he obtains. One might conclude, therefore, that if we wish to divert travelers from the automobile to transit, using natural market forces rather than artificial incentives or punitive measures, it will be necessary to provide a competitive level of service in the transit system. The fact that the auto tripmaker already pays a high price for the quality of service he obtains suggests that he would be willing to pay similar amounts for competitive services offered by a public system.

Efficiency of Free Transit Subsidy

To evaluate free transit service, it is necessary to examine its effectiveness in achieving given objectives in comparison with the efficiency of meeting these objectives by other means.

The goals commonly presented in arguments for free transit service include the following:

1. To improve the accessibility of job opportunities for ghetto residents.
2. To aid in revitalizing the downtowns.
3. To divert auto travelers to transit, and thereby reduce mounting rush-hour highway congestion, decrease air pollution, and reduce the demand for parking facilities.

We will discuss each of these objectives in turn.

Improve Accessibility of Jobs to Ghetto Residents

It has frequently been suggested that transit subsidies be used to aid residents of the central city slums or ghettos, often nonwhite minority groups with low incomes and poor educational backgrounds whose residential choices are largely limited by housing segregation to the ghetto area. At the same time many of the

---

[g]A. Scheffer Lang and Richard M. Soberman, *Urban Rail Transit: Its Economics and Technology*, M.I.T. Press, Cambridge, Massachusetts, 1964, p. 90.

service, retailing, and lesser skilled manufacturing jobs for which they tend to be presently best suited are rapidly dispersing to the outlying areas. These residents often find that urban transportation systems considerably add to their isolation and their economic problems. Car ownership is often unrealistic given the parking and insurance costs and this group's income level, yet the lack of adequate public transportation is often a substantial barrier to commuting outward to work or even to learning about job opportunities. The transit system often provides reasonable service only for the radial trip pattern that was predominant several decades ago rather than for the cross-city trips which are now needed to move ghetto residents to dispersed job opportunities. Good transit service is usually available from the ghetto to the downtown area, but the service to the now dispersed job areas is often indirect, infrequent, and extremely time-consuming.

The efficiency of free transit in dealing with this situation is doubtful from several aspects. First, the use of the transportation system as a welfare mechanism is itself questionable. If the goal of the program is to redistribute income, it is generally conceded to be more efficient to make direct income payments to the recipients rather than payments in kind. Furthermore, making all transit services free is an extremely expensive way to subsidize ghetto residents, because high-income as well as low-income people would receive the subsidy. If the goal of free transit is to subsidize low-income ghetto residents, it would be much less costly to restrict free service to the low income population. There are a number of administrative mechanisms for doing this, such as collecting the fares in the residential areas for all trips and collecting none (and providing free transfers) in the ghetto areas.

Second, as a practical matter, it is difficult to see how eliminating the fare in the present systems will significantly reduce the isolation of the ghettos. Too often the basic problem is that the transit systems do not provide adequate service from the ghettos to dispersed job locations. Making the existing service free will not correct this problem.

A more effective approach is to provide improved transit service from the ghettos to job centers. This service could be made free to ghetto residents for far less than the subsidy needed to finance completely free service; or users could be charged for the service on the theory that the job is not worth having if it does not provide for the worker's cost of transportation.

In the Boston case study, we located the low-income residential areas and the low-skilled job centers and estimated the cost of providing very good bus service between the residential areas and the job centers.[h] Peak-hour headways were held to fifteen minutes or less except for express service to industrial parks, where they were uniformly thirty minutes. The one-way running times never exceeded thirty minutes except for the express service to industrial parks, which ranged from thirty to forty minutes.

The collection and distribution systems were very extensive so that all ghetto residents were put within one-fourth mile or less of a bus line and most job locations were very close to a bus stop. Little or no transferring was required.

[h]The low-income residential centers were identified from the 1960 Census tract reports. We defined low income as 1959 median family incomes of less than $4500 per year, but we also included areas of Dorchester occupied since 1960 by black people. The job centers were located by means of the Greater Boston Chamber of Commerce, *Directory of Manufacturers in Greater Boston, 1966-1967,* (Boston, 1967).

In contrast, the ghetto areas in Boston are now provided very poor service to almost all job locations except the downtown area. Trip times are commonly two to three times greater than those provided by the service improvements evaluated in the case study, or service is so slow and roundabout as to be prohibitively expensive in time and money.

The new service consists of forty-two new bus routes, thirty local and twelve express. The new routes comprise 310.6 added route miles (one-way), of which 102.2 are local and 208.4 are express. They require 165 additional vehicles and 245 additional men. Total annual bus mileage operated is 2,390,000 miles.

The estimated cost of these service improvements was approximately $4.3 million per year (for both operating costs and capital recovery).[i] This is only about 6 percent of the estimated annual cost for free transit service for the Boston area. Thus, providing service improvements for ghetto residents appears to be a far more effective means of improving their accessibility to jobs than a program of free transit. This service need not be offered free, but if it is made free to ghetto users, it would require only a small fraction of the cost of a comprehensive free transit program.

A similar line of reasoning emerges when assistance to other disadvantaged groups is examined. For example, free transit service is a very inefficient means of meeting the transportation needs of the aged and handicapped. If the needs of that group are to be subsidized, it is undoubtedly cheaper to provide taxis or jitneys than to provide a complete program of free transit for all users. Moreover, since the present transit equipment is usually poorly designed for boarding and discharging elderly or handicapped passengers, a program of free transit fails to meet one of the basic needs of these people, which is service tailored to their physical limitations.

Revitalize the Downtown

It is a familiar story that there has been a profound change in the relative importance of central cities in the postwar period. Retail sales, employment, and population of the central cities have either declined or remained roughly constant, while enormous growth has occurred in the metropolitan areas outside the central cities. Ganz shows that in the twenty-four largest metropolitan areas, central city employment remained almost constant from 1948 to 1963 as gains in service employment were almost completely offset by declines in trade and manufacturing. At the same time, the portions of the metropolitan areas outside the central cities almost doubled in employment.[j]

This dispersion was stimulated by a variety of forces. Higher incomes, the greater mobility arising from improved highway facilities and increased car ownership, and the desire for low density housing stimulated residential dispersion. Job dispersion was stimulated by the economics of one-story plants and improved communications and transportation facilities which reduced the need for physical proximity. The dispersion of retail activity was stimulated by

[i]The costs are distributed as follows

Labor	$2.6 million
Mileage	1.0
Equipment	0.7
Total	$4.3 million

[j]Alexander Ganz, *Emerging Patterns of Urban Growth and Travel*, M.I.T. Project Transport, January 1968.

the residential dispersion of customers and the development of one-story retail shopping centers as a means of providing adequate parking space and good accessibility to highways. The relative importance of these factors is not at all well understood, but fundamental economic and technological changes underlie the trend toward decentralization.

In the face of these basic technological and economic forces, it may be very difficult and costly to preserve the downtown in its traditional role and it may even be impossible or undesirable to do so. The growth in service employment coupled with decreases in trade and manufacturing suggest, however, that some forms of activity find the downtown location economic even though other activities are dispersing. Activities drawing upon very large segments of the population may require the centralization obtainable by central business district location; those activities that can achieve sufficiently large markets in the suburban areas might best avoid central business district locations. The central business district may be appropriate as a location for highly specialized retailing; art galleries; cultural activities such as theaters, exhibition halls, and museums; financial activities, and government functions. Rather than trying to preserve the past functions of the downtown by subsidizing uneconomic trade and manufacturing activities through a program of publicly supported mass transit service, it may be more appropriate to try to stimulate the growth of those activities for which the central business district is an economic location and give up those activities which are now better suited to low density areas.

Nevertheless, it is reasonable to examine the relative effectiveness of a program of free transit service as a means of stimulating downtown activity. The demand model indicates that free transit would increase downtown shopping trips by about one-third. The zero cross-elasticity in the demand model suggests that the fare reduction would not decrease automobile shopping trips. This suggests that rather than diverting trips from suburban shopping centers to the downtown, the free fare would simply increase transit trips. The new trips could be made by shoppers who previously walked or they could be an increase in the number of shopping trips made by persons already using transit. In the latter case, this could represent less carefully planned shopping trips as a result of a reduction in the money cost of an additional trip. It is questionable whether the increase in trips would result in a sizeable increase in downtown sales if there is no diversion from suburban shopping centers. It is possible that with free transit, some shopping would be done that would not be done otherwise, but one would expect the amount to be small. Also, we would expect some diversion to the downtown from secondary urban shopping areas as the fare inducement should attract some shoppers who now walk to neighborhood centers.

From a cost-effectiveness viewpoint, it may be more efficient to subsidize service improvements rather than fares. Our estimates show that for transit shopping trips the elasticity of demand with respect to savings in time is about twice as great as the fare elasticity. The effect on auto shopping trips (*i.e.*, the cross-elasticity), however, is near zero.

We calculated the cost of adding service (*i.e.*, improving the collection and distribution system to reduce non-line-haul travel time) where the effect of service improvements could be measured relatively easily. By this we mean we examined improvements to existing routes but not increased geographical coverage, such as new routes to provide service for cross-city trips. The effect of increased geographic coverage is difficult to measure because it is not possible simply to compute the estimated change in volume from the existing service as can be done with improvements to existing routes. Instead, it is necessary to obtain the values of the socioeconomic variables of the affected origin and destination zones together with all the travel time and cost information by both auto and the new transit service and then compute the volume of transit traffic. In short, there is no existing base of transit ridership from which changes can be measured.

In improving the service of existing routes, new capacity was provided to reduce the walk, wait, and transfer times, and through service was provided in many cases to avoid the inconvenience of one or more transfers. The entire population now served by the MBTA was put within one-fourth mile of a bus line. No line operated less frequently than every ten minutes in the peak hours. All bus lines lying within a few miles of the CBD were extended to serve the CBD directly. Express bus services were inaugurated on lines to outlying areas.

These service improvements required fifty-nine additional local routes and twenty additional express bus routes. The local routes comprised 207.4 one-way route miles, while the express bus service consisted of 153.6 additional one-way route miles. Total new vehicles required were 385, while 592 additional operators were needed. Annual operating mileage was 8,390,000 miles.

The annual cost of these improvements was estimated to be $12 million, distributed as follows:

Labor	$6.2 million
Mileage	4.2
Equipment	1.6
Total	$12.0 million

In computing these costs we assumed an annual wage per operator, including benefits, of $10,500; variable cost per mile of operation of $.50 (somewhat higher than the present $.41 in spite of express bus operations because of the probable need for an increase in overhead with such a large expansion of service); and an annual equipment cost based on twelve years expected life, 6 percent cost of capital, zero scrap value, and original cost of $34,000 per bus.

These service improvements reduced transit excess times on the existing systems by about 25 percent overall. Based on the demand model and the reductions in travel time we estimate that these service improvements would increase transit shopping trips to the downtown on the order of 15 percent, with no reduction in auto trips. Moreover, the added capacity would reduce the load factors on nearly every existing MBTA line. This would reduce overcrowding in the rush hours, provide more room for packages, increase the probability of getting a seat, and so forth. These service improvements would provide an additional stimulus to transit shopping trips. The added trips arising from the lower load factors cannot be estimated from the demand model, so the 15 percent figure is an underestimate of the expected increase in transit shopping trips.

In summary, about half of the stimulus of the free-fare subsidy to Boston shopping could be achieved for less than one-sixth of the cost by allocating the subsidy funds to service improvements. This result stems partly from directing the subsidy toward a more limited objective and partly from the greater responsiveness of the shoppers to service improvements than to fares.

Based on our estimated travel demand functions, the strongest inducement to downtown shopping is likely to be cheap and convenient parking. The demand elasticities with respect to these aspects of the auto shopping trip are four to five times higher than the transit fare elasticity.[k] It is also important to recognize that auto shopping trips attracted to the downtown by good parking facilities are in part diverted from suburban shopping centers and therefore are likely to result in an increase in downtown sales rather than simply an increase in the number of trips to the downtown. The relative effectiveness of parking facilities in stimulating sales probably accounts in large part for the observed tendency of downtown merchants to build or lease parking facilities for their customers rather than banding together to provide free downtown transit service.

Reduce Highway Congestion,
Air Pollution, Parking Problems

It is popularly believed that urban highway congestion, particularly in the peak hours, is growing worse over time. As mentioned earlier, the facts on this are fragmentary, but they provide no compelling evidence that urban auto congestion is increasing,[l] and, in fact, the opposite seems more likely to be true. Although there has been a tremendous increase in auto ownership in recent years — the number of automobiles in use roughly doubled over the 1950-1966 period, from 35 million in 1950 to 71 million in 1966[m] — there have also been large additions to urban highway capacity. These highway capacity additions coupled with the reduction in travel demands in the core city as a result of job and residence dispersion have resulted in highway performance at the peak hours which seems to be at least as good today as a decade ago, and a considerable improvement over that in the immediate postwar years. In most cities auto trip times have actually fallen slightly over this period. The peak period in the day, that period during which auto congestion is greatest, has also narrowed somewhat.

[k]The elasticity of demand for shopping trips with respect to auto out-of-pocket cost and excess time are -1.65 and -1.44.

[l]For a discussion of the evidence on this point see J.R. Meyer, *et. al., op. cit.,* pp. 74-82.

[m]U.S. Bureau of the Census, *Statistical Abstract of the United States, 1967,* Washington, D.C., p. 566.

The performance of most urban highway systems does fall far short of the expectations of many travelers, but the data suggest that this is more likely to be due to unfilled hopes than to a deterioration in performance. Construction of an urban freeway leads people to expect free-flowing traffic on the freeway at the posted speed limits all hours of the day. During rush hours, the performance of the freeway is considerably less than this; and travelers find it difficult to believe that the new freeway has contributed anything to the reduction of congestion and delay. Part of the heavy traffic on the new freeway is new travel induced by the addition of the freeway; part is traffic diverted from paralleling arterials. Thus, to examine the effects of the new freeway on auto congestion it is necessary to consider also the reduction in peak-hour congestion on paralleling arterials. The available evidence from Chicago, Boston, and Los Angeles suggests that when travel times over the entire corridor are examined, urban freeways have considerably reduced peak-hour congestion on the arterials and improved the performance of the urban highway system accordingly. Nevertheless, the popular dissatisfaction with highway performance has lent considerable urgency to various proposals to reduce auto congestion further.

The effectiveness of a program of free transit to reduce auto congestion further depends on the cross-elasticity of auto demand with respect to transit fares. The appropriate trip purpose to examine for the morning peak is the work trip, while in the afternoon peak, nonwork trips are also important. The afternoon peak is now generally higher and of longer duration than the morning peak.

Our statistical analysis of demand indicates that most of the increase in rush-hour transit work trips brought about by a fare decrease would be diverted from automobile travel. The direct transit elasticity and the auto cross-elasticity are about the same, the number of peak-hour auto and transit travelers in Boston proper are almost equal, and the number of work trips as a percentage of total trips is not greatly different for the two modes. For nonwork trips, on the other hand, there is virtually no diversion from auto; all the additional transit trips are induced trips. These results seem reasonable for work trips as it is unlikely that a fare reduction will cause people to increase their total number of work trips. For nonwork trips, it is unreasonable to believe that some diversion from auto would not occur, although the diversion may very well be small. Thus, our results probably understate the diversion in nonwork auto traffic somewhat, but they suggest that transit fare reductions are unlikely to reduce nonwork auto trips in an important way and are likely to be a very inefficient means of trying to do so.

Our estimate shows that a zero fare would increase transit work trips by about 17 percent and lower auto work trips by about 14 percent. To convert the 14 percent reduction in auto work trips to total auto trips, it is necessary to multiply by the fraction of auto work trips to total auto trips. The rush-hour ratio of auto work trips to total auto trips is about 0.66 in the morning peak and 0.40 in the evening peak.[n]

This adjustment gives a reduction in morning rush-hour traffic of about 9 percent and in the evening peak of about 6 percent.

[n] These figures were compiled from the trip tables of the 1963 Wilbur Smith and Associates home interview survey in the Boston area.

Again, a more efficient means of reducing rush-hour auto traffic appears to be to improve transit service (*i.e.*, reduce non-line-haul travel times by improving the collection and distribution system). This follows from our estimates of cross-elasticities. The auto cross-elasticity with respect to transit non-line-haul time is more than 2.5 times the cross-elasticity with respect to fares (0.373 versus 0.138). As mentioned above, we calculated the cost of improving the collection and distribution service in Boston where service improvements could be measured relatively easily. For an annual cost of about $12 million we found that non-line-haul transit times could be reduced by about 25 percent. According to our demand model this would reduce auto work trips by about 9 percent (*i.e.*, 0.373 x 0.25). The peak-hour reductions in total auto traffic from the improved service would be about 6 percent in the morning rush and about 4 percent in the evening. Thus, two-thirds of the reduction in auto traffic could be obtained for about one-sixth of the cost of free transit.

The automobile is a major contributor to air pollution problems in our large urban centers. The effects on air quality of diverting trips from auto to transit are difficult to quantify with any precision, but rough approximations can be made.[o] There are two important aspects to consider: automobile emissions and the effect of the emissions on ambient air quality. While measurements of emissions have been made under fairly controlled conditions, it is much more difficult to measure their effects on ambient air quality. These vary with meteorological conditions and the distribution of emission sources.

Automobiles emit three pollutants in quantity: hydrocarbons, carbon monoxide, and oxides of nitrogen. While there are very limited data on the effects of these combustion products on life and property, it is known, for example, that hydrocarbons and oxides of nitrogen combine in the presence of sunlight to produce photochemical smog — a major irritant and source of human discomfort.

Gasoline-powered vehicles are the source of approximately 85 percent of the hydrocarbons, 95 percent of the carbon monoxide, and 30 percent of the oxides of nitrogen in New England. The figures given are for all gasoline-powered vehicles in the six-state New England area, *i.e.*, passenger cars, trucks, and buses in both urban and rural areas. They are not significant contributors to sulfur dioxide emissions and particulates, the other principal air pollutants. Table 6-1 presents the 1965 national levels of vehicle miles for automobiles, trucks, and buses. Although the emissions depend on the type of fuel used in combustion, the bulk of the fuel consumed is gasoline, *i.e.*, only about 5 percent of the highway vehicle fuel consumed in diesel (or other non-gasoline fuels), and most of this is consumed by trucks in rural service. According to the Bureau of Public Roads, 1965 fuel consumption in miles per gallon was 14.3 for passenger vehicles excluding buses, 5.4 for buses, and 8.5 for trucks. Unfortunately, these are highly aggregative figures with no detail being given for urban versus rural service or for gasoline versus diesel fuel. Nevertheless, they are useful for establishing orders of magnitude for our purposes. Table 6-2 presents an estimated distribution of fuel consumption using these gross rates.

[o]The following discussion is based on *Economic Impact of Environmental Control and Management in New England,* Charles River Associates, Incorporated, Cambridge, Massachusetts, June 1968. This study of the economics of air, water, and solid waste pollution was prepared for the New England Regional Commission.

Table 6-1

**U. S. Motor Vehicle Travel By Type
of Vehicle and Type of Area, 1965
(billions of vehicle-miles)**

	Urban	Rural	Total[1]
Passenger cars, motorcycles, and taxicabs	357	353	709
Buses	2	3	5
Trucks and combinations	65	109	174
Total	424	465	888

[1] Total may not add due to rounding.

Source: *Statistical Abstract of the United States — 1967,* U. S. Department of Commerce. Data are referenced to the Department of Transportation, Bureau of Public Roads.

Table 6-2

**Estimated Fuel Consumption in U. S.
Motor Vehicle Transportation, 1965
(billions of gallons)**

	Urban	Rural	Total[1]
Passenger cars, motorcycles, taxicabs	25.0	24.7	49.6
Buses	.4	.6	.9
Trucks and combinations	7.6	12.8	20.5
Total	33.0	38.1	71.0

[1] Totals may not add due to rounding.

Free or improved transit will not affect the volume of rural automobile travel. As indicated by the figures in Table 6-2, urban automobile travel consumes about 35 percent of the fuel in the country as a whole and about 76 percent of the fuel in the urban areas.

If we make the assumption that automobile emissions are roughly proportional to the fuel consumed,[p] it is possible to calculate the effect of free transit. In Boston we estimate a 14 percent reduction in automobile work trips resulting from free transit, with no corresponding net change in nonwork trips. In the Boston area 37 percent of all auto trips are work trips.[q] Since 76 percent of the urban highway vehicle emissions are from the automobile, the reduction in vehicular emissions resulting from free transit would be about 4 percent (*i.e.*, 0.14 x 0.37 x 0.76 = 0.04), ignoring any increased pollution from greater use of transit vehicles. It is unlikely that such a reduction will have much effect on ambient air quality. The reduction may be important if the pollutants are concentrated in the most congested areas and even more so if the effects are nonlinear, but there is some limited evidence that the concentration disperses over a fairly large area around the source.

To place this estimated reduction in emissions in greater perspective, it should be noted that the control devices automobile models for 1968 and later, when properly maintained, will reduce emissions of hydrocarbons and of carbon monoxide by about two-thirds as compared with earlier model cars without exhaust control. These devices do not reduce the emissions of oxides of nitrogen. It is important to add that the consumption of each gallon of diesel fuel by buses produces nearly twice the oxides of nitrogen as a gallon of gasoline (although the emission levels for the other pollutants are lower). In addition, diesel engines emit particulate pollutants and odors which may be offensive.

Even if the entire automobile emission is highly concentrated in the central urban areas, the 4 percent reduction resulting from free transit may simply delay slightly the deterioration of ambient air quality. Urban auto travel has been increasing at something over 4 percent annually. This would imply a delay of less than a year, although some of this growth in travel may be due to the expanding size of the urban areas so the assumption of concentration is probably not valid. In any event, the potential for improving the ambient air quality through the introduction of free transit appears to be slight.

Improvements in air quality will probably be best accomplished by means other than free transit. Improvements in transit service may have greater impact on air pollution by diverting larger volumes of automobile trips, but the effects on air quality will still probably be insignificant compared to the improvement that can be obtained by controlling the emissions themselves.

The reduction in auto travel resulting from the diversion of auto trips to transit will reduce parking requirements, particularly in the downtown areas. Because the principal diversion resulting from free transit will be auto work trips, the significance of the effect is increased. The desirable number of parking spaces for each CBD work trip by auto is estimated to be .5; for each CBD nonwork trip the estimate is .147.[r] These figures, which appear to be reasonable,

[p]This assumption is frequently made.

[q]Wilbur Smith and Associates, 1963 home interview survey.

[r]Wilbur Smith and Associates, *Parking in* *the City Center*, New Haven, Connecticut, May 1965, p. 22. These figures are not given for any specific city and the report indicates that there may be some variability depending on the area's characteristics.

are based on considerations of car occupancy, parking turnover for trips of various purposes, and the efficiency of parking space usage. For example, if average car occupancy is 1.5 and the vehicles were parked for the entire day, .667 parking spaces would be required per person trip. Some work trips, of course, do not require all day parking, and certainly nonwork trips do not generally park all day. In fact, although there are no specific data available, one might reasonably expect that those work trips diverted from transit are likely to be trips with very low parking turnover. Work trips, for example, made by business men whose jobs require travel during the day are unlikely to be diverted to transit. As a result the figure of .5 parking spaces per work trip is probably too high when evaluating the effect on parking of auto diversion to transit.

Because of the differences in parking turnover between work and nonwork auto trips, the reduction of one auto work trip may provide parking space for at least 3.4 nonwork trips.[s] In some places this may simply provide parking spaces where there is already a shortage, or some or all of the reduction in requirements may be used to achieve other benefits, such as improving traffic flows by eliminating curb parking.

The increase in parking spaces available for nonwork tripmakers will have additional stimulating effects. The demand for shopping trips, for example, is elastic with respect to the cost and convenience of parking.[t] The availability of increased parking facilities through diversion of auto work trips to transit will reduce out-of-vehicle time.

Approximately 70,000 daily work trips by auto are destined to downtown Boston from areas outside downtown but within the metropolitan area. Similarly there are approximately 90,000 daily nonwork trips by auto. Using the parking requirement parameters given by the Wilbur Smith study, it would be desirable to have 48,000 parking spaces. It is estimated that the introduction of free transit would divert 14 percent of the auto work trips. This would result in a reduction of about 10,000 downtown auto work trips and a corresponding release of approximately 5,000 downtown parking spaces, not including any factor for differences in parking turnover between diverted and nondiverted trips. Again using the Wilbur Smith parameters, the release of 5,000 downtown parking spaces for work trips would accommodate an additional 34,000 nonwork trips, an increase of nearly 40 percent.[u] Of course, such calculations are extremely crude but the orders of magnitude are revealing.

[s]That is $0.5 \div 0.147 = 3.4$.

[t]This elasticity of demand for shopping trips with respect to out-of-vehicle time, *i. e.,* time to walk from the parking place to the destination, is estimated to be -1.44; for out-of-pocket cost, it is -1.65.

[u]Although according to the formula, the entire downtown Boston area has approximately the desired number of parking spaces, it would be hard to convince anyone familiar with the downtown Boston area of this fact. This is undoubtedly in part due to a poor geographic distribution of these spaces within the downtown area. According to the Boston Redevelopment Authority in *Transportation Facts for the Boston Region,* 1967 edition, p. 63, there are 47,860 spaces in downtown Boston including 25,004 public off-street, 14,722 curb spaces and 8,134 spaces for public use. In addition, there are about 17,000 illegal curb spaces that are frequently in use.

These results show that diversion of auto trips to transit will have a significant impact on parking in the downtown area. Although such diversion may result from the elimination of transit fares, as discussed earlier this diversion may be obtained at far lower cost to society by the improvement of transit service levels.

7

Some Administrative and Financial Considerations

In this chapter we shall discuss some of the administrative problems involved in providing a system of free transit, including the financing and income redistributional considerations which would arise in any program of public subsidy to transit.

Subsidy Administration

A free transit subsidy program will present difficult administrative problems, stemming primarily from the lack of market information that is usually obtained from prices. When charges are made for service, the administrator can infer that the value of the service to the user is at least equal to the price paid. If revenues cover the costs of providing the service, he knows that the resources used up in providing it do not exceed the worth of the service to the public. By weighing revenues against costs, the administrator can determine whether the value to society of some component of service is more or less than its cost.[a] Both prices and service levels can be adjusted until the appropriate level of expenditures is determined. With free transit, as in any public investment program based on other than "market" benefits or other obvious indices of the worth of expenditures, a means must be devised by which the net benefits of public investment are measured and evaluated so that a rational allocation of resources can be determined.

There are four aspects to the problem: determining the initial operating budgets for the different metropolitan areas; specifying criteria for making spending decisions within a given operating budget; developing a means by which administrators can assess the results of any program; and providing guidelines for expansion or curtailment of services as cities grow or transportation needs change.

To determine the initial operating budget for a metropolitan area, it is logical to start with the current budgets. As mentioned earlier, however, these may not reflect the replacement costs of new equipment and, therefore, service would tend to deteriorate over time in many cities unless subsidies were somewhat larger than current budgets. In addition, the current budgets cover the costs of the route structures, schedule frequencies, equipment configurations, etc. of the present transit systems and it is by no means clear that these are in close conformity with the market's demand for service and that they should form the basis for allocating subsidy funds. In this regard, it is necessary to consider the disparity in current service levels among cities. If communities do not directly

---

[a]This assumes, of course, that external costs are also considered. Thus, full social costs must be taken into account.

incur the costs of their transit service, there is likely to be a tendency for all cities to want the best level of service available, regardless of their existing level.

Criteria for making spending decisions within a given budget are very difficult to determine in the absence of price information. Market fares and ridership typically provide important information in guiding management decisions as to system design, the choice of routes, and service levels, even though present pricing by no means closely conforms to costs on all components of the typical transit system and there are distortions form rational investment, routing, and service levels. Furthermore, while there may be external or social consequences of transit or highway system operations not adequately reflected in the market, to recognize their existence is a far cry from choosing to be deprived of all market information by instituting a zero fare system.

Rational administration of a program as large as that being considered almost certainly means direction from the state and local levels. Open-ended grants such as the present capital grant program obtain administrative simplicity by foregoing any process of supervision over each component expenditure. However, a program of subsidy directed at particular routes or types of routes within an urban transportation system would be an impossible task to administer at the federal level; it would, for example, make the administrative difficulties of the Civil Aeornautics Board's subsidy program to local service air carriers pale by comparison. Supervision of an operating cost subsidy program is not easily achieved. A local program − perhaps a federal-local tax sharing arrangement in which local administrators are primarily responsible for contracting with local transit authorities for the services desired − is most likely to be effective.

A program in which transit operators are paid on a contract basis for agreed-upon services, with the contractor determining the most efficient means of providing the services, may be the best administrative device, although defining the output so purchased would be very difficult. Inappropriate criteria − for example, so much subsidy per seat mile − might induce transit operators to neglect consumers' wishes and provide excessive service during off-peak hours or on low-density routes where the highest provision of "capacity" can be recorded. In general, any subsidy scheme which results in a disparity between operators' incentives and ridership demand is likely to result in inappropriate or poor service. Conversely, paying so much per passenger carried could induce operators to serve only the densest routes and to offer short-haul service conducive to more transfers and hence more passengers. Such a procedure would also require continuous accounting of ridership − an accounting which might be a temptation for fraud. The thrust of these remarks is to suggest that it is not easy to structure a subsidy program which captures both the incentives inplicit in a market system and the responsibility of management.

Another fundamental concern in instituting a public subsidy program involves the likely effects on management and labor incentives; in particular, the risk that public subsidy will reduce the incentive to operate effeciently. Means must be found for retaining cost control and for avoiding union relationships which limit the introduction of labor-saving technology. Since labor costs are such a substantial percentage of transit operating costs, the role of unions and the likely effects of public subsidy on labor-management practices is an especially serious issue. The experience of the operating subsidy paid to certain U. S. merchant marine operations by the Maritime Administration is a vivid reminder. Under this program the U. S. government pays all labor costs above the prevailing world wage rate to U. S. seamen so employed. Thus the general public, which pays all of any wage increases agreed upon, is not really represented when the maritime unions and management bargain for new wage contracts. As a result of the program, wage rates and labor inputs are higher than found in nonsubsidized maritime operations.

In general, legitimate concern can be raised about the possibility that in a subsidy program as large as that implied by a free fare system for all present mass transit systems, inertia could develop which would lead over time to poor market performance. A large subsidy program will create substantial vested interest by transit labor, management, and certain groups of riders, presenting a considerable challenge to the political and administrative processes which shape the net results of such a program. A subsidy program might well become "institutionalized" and the regulatory or support process become closely wedded to a mutual interest with the industry participants. As another example, it is not unlikely that a certain rigidity might develop with regard to new routings or service levels on particular routes. In view of the considerable and rapid changes in city shape and the associated pattern of trips, this sort of rigidity (which is already present in varying degrees in many cities) would be very undesirable.

Income Transfers

One of the most significant aspects of a subsidized transit system is the method of raising the revneue to finance the operation. Free transit may be free to the users, but it certainly cannot be regarded as free to society. Transit requires substantial resources which must be diverted from other uses. Regardless of how these resources are paid for, the method of financing may create transfers of income from one group in society to another. Perhaps only in the case where each user of the service pays the long-run cost of the incremental resources provided him and aggregate revenues equal total costs can there be general agreement that there is no income transfer. Unless both conditions are fulfilled, transfers will necessarily take place.

Even where total revenues equal total costs under a single flat fare system if costs vary between services, with some users paying more than their incremental cost and others paying less, there is a transfer from those paying more to those paying less. This type of cross-subsidy is not at all uncommon in transportation, and mass transportation is no exception to the practice. In general, fares are not sufficiently tapered as a function of distance and density to reflect the cost economies of shorter and denser routes. Lower density routes to distant suburbs are usually underpriced compared to heavily traveled routes in the core city. To the extent that incomes are correlated with distance from the CBD and thereby with the length of a commuting transit trip, this form of cross-subsidization imposes a burden on those with low incomes. This circumstance is the result both of political pressures exerted by "suburbia" and collection costs entailed by pricing systems more elaborate than payment of a single fare. Transit companies have not been quick to adopt "zone fares," a procedure whereby fares rise in stages with trip distance. While methods are available to institute these more complex fare structures, there has long been resistance to innovations in fare collection procedures. The consequences of any transit support program on the income distribution are intimately related to the way in which the service is priced. When revenues do not equal costs, some form of support is required if the operation is to be continued. In evaluating the distributional consequences of any method of providing the support, there are three general types of income transfers to be considered: redistributions of income between users and nonusers, redistributions among regions, and redistributions from one socio-economic class to another. These transfers are very difficult to quantify and we make no attempt to do so here. Moreover, conventional economics can provide no objective judgment on the merits or demerits of various transfers; of necessity their evaluation lies in the political sphere.

To the extent transit subsidies are provided from any form of general or broad-based taxation there is an income transfer from nonusers to users, that is, the transit rider obtains the use of resources at a price that is less than the cost of providing them, and thus has an implicit increase in his income. Taxpayers pay the difference between the cost and revenue. The nonuser obtains no service for his tax payment, and hence has a decrease in his income. So long as the tax incidence does not fall solely on the user such a transfer will take place. Where present systems operate at a deficit financed by local taxes, this type of transfer exists today. To make such subsidies more prevalent through a reduction or complete elimination of fares will increase the amount of this transfer.

If the tax base for the subsidy is broader than the local area served by the transit system, regional redistribution occurs. State or federal tax financing of local transit operations redistributes income from rural and small urban areas without transit service to larger urban areas where the services are provided. This sort of transfer would certainly occur with a program of free transit financed out of general tax revenues. Regional redistribution also occurs if some of the districts served by the transit system are provided more service than they pay for. A redistribution of this sort was described above. Lower density suburban routes are often underpriced and receive a cross-subsidy from high density routes in the core city. Because most transit systems are heavily oriented to the CBD, a free transit program financed out of general tax funds would benefit downtown merchants and residents at the expense of secondary and suburban shopping centers and residents of outlying areas if the tax incidence did not compensate for the differences in service.

Finally, where the socioeconomic distribution of users is different from the distribution of the tax incidence, there is an income redistribution between socioeconomic classes. Such is the case, for example, when local taxes falling on low income groups are used to subsidize the services provided high income suburban riders. To the extent that federal taxes are more progressive than state or municipal taxes, subsidies paid out of federal funds may result in politically more desirable transfers between socioeconomic groups. Nevertheless, persons with relatively low incomes do pay taxes and some of their taxes will go toward the subsidy even when the federal tax system is used.

An obvious alternative to appropriate user charges or to financing transit subsidies out of general taxation is the imposition of the tax as directly as possible on those who will receive the benefits. For example, if the motive of free transit service is to preserve the CBD, a tax on downtown residents and merchants may be appropriate. Such a recommendation may not be acceptable to downtown residents and mayors who would, quite rightly, point to their considerable other public finance programs and argue that additional assessments would only heighten the trend toward decentralization. On the other hand, it is probably not reasonable to expect a willingness of outlying area residents and merchants to pay taxes which subsidize shopping and other activities downtown, sometimes complementing but often in competition with the suburban taxpayer.

8   Additional Research Needs

It seems clear that the important task is to improve urban transportation planning in general. Recommendations for future research, therefore, should be designed to improve our basic knowledge of urban transportation, rather than simply to enable a more precise and refined evaluation to be made of free transit, which is only one approach among many meriting serious consideration.

To improve urban transportation planning, the overwhelming needs for additional research are in the areas of passenger demand and the relationship between urban development and transportation facilities. The need is widely recognized for a method of projecting urban transportation demand under a variety of different assumptions about the price, speed, frequency and convenience of service, etc., of different transportation modes. Indeed, the need for research on transportation demands goes beyond this and includes such areas as the possible effects of new technology, the interrelationships between transportation systems and land-use patterns, and the possibliity of adapting urban transportation planning to larger social objectives. Additional research on system cost and performance is also needed, but is probably less urgent than the need for additional study of demand simply because more research has already been done on costing and performance.

The model presented in Chapter 2 is the first urban transportation demand model that expresses meaningful causal relationships. Without estimates of these behavioral relationships, it is impossible to learn what transportation improvements the public wants, and without that information there can be no effective system design because designers must be able to understand and respond to the needs of the users.

Although we feel that the demand model used for this study is a substantial improvement over the conventional models developed in connection with the typical urban transportation project, it is, nevertheless still very primitive. The most important shortcomings were discussed in Chapter 2. These are the aggregation of all transit modes into one heterogeneous transit mode, the lack of time-of-day distinctions, and the static assumption that land-use is not influenced by the transportation system. All three limitations need to be overcome.

In view of the interest and resources being devoted to the development and implementation of new technologies and systems for public transportation, we believe that it is very important to have an understanding of the separate effects of the different transit modes. Overcoming the heterogeneous transit mode is relatively simple. It requires obtaining a data tape with unlinked trips, redefining the linked trips, and reestimating the model. The increase in modes, however, will add to already formidable collinearity and estimation problems, so additional care will be required in sample selection, model specification, and choice of estimation technique.

The inclusion of time-of-day elasticity would include in the model the decision of when to travel. This is important because, just as it is possible to reduce rush-hour congestion (to some extent) by diverting travelers from one mode to another, or one route to another, it is also possible to divert some travelers from one hour to another. Virtually nothing is known quantitatively about the possibilities of this type of diversion. According to the Boston data, about two-thirds of the morning (7:00—9:00 A.M.) and 40 percent of the evening (4:00—6:00 P.M.) rush-hour auto trips are work trips. Most of these are constrained to present times of travel by the job arrival and departure times. A portion of the remaining one-third of the morning rush-hour trips are school trips which are also so constrained. However, the majority of trips in the afternoon peak and a sizeable number of morning rush-hour trips are nonwork trips, some portion of which could be shifted to off-peak hours. It is possible that a significant number of these travelers could be diverted to off-peak travel by implementation of suitable policy measures, for instance, differential toll and fare structures. However, at this time little or nothing is known about the response of travelers to these incentives.

As with the inclusion of additional modes in the model, the inclusion of several times of day would substantially complicate the model and make estimation very difficult. However, data are presently available in machine processable form to investigate the inclusion of both additional transit modes and the time-of-day elasticities.

A model is badly needed of the relationship between the transportation system and land use. Over time, congestion on the transportation system can be partially relieved by adaptations in land use. For example, if trips become too time-consuming because of growing traffic levels, some workers may change their residential locations (or firms may relocate) to reduce travel times, thereby alleviating some of the congestion on the system. This sort of land use adjustment may be an acceptable alternative to adding cross-town freeway capacity, particularly if these self-adapting adjustments take place in a reasonable period of time.

Similarly, additions to transportation system capacity will, over time, cause changes in land use that will in turn affect the levels of traffic in the system. A new highway link, for example, may in time stimulate much more travel than would be indicated by the static demand model used in this study. In addition to increasing travel by the existing households served by the new link, it would stimulate additional land use development which in time might also increase travel on the link.

To evaluate transportation investment alternatives, therefore, a quantitative understanding must be developed of the interaction between the transportation system and urban development. To be fully useful, the model should measure the time lags involved in the adjustment of land use to changes in the transportation system; that is, the model should be dynamic.

Since the time response of urban development to changes in the transportation system cannot be captured by a cross-sectional analysis made at one point in time, time series data are needed. The required data are the transportation system performance characteristics, inventories of land-use, and origin destination trip data. Gathering the necessary data will be costly and time consuming. One of the mistakes that has been made in collecting urban transportation data in the past is that questionnaires have been prepared and the data collected before the model for which the data were to be used was designed. As a result, essential data were overlooked and much of the available data could only be used with difficulty. Effective and efficient data collection cannot take place in a vacuum. Because of the excessive cost and long lead times involved in developing the data base for investigating the interrelationship between the transportation system and urban development, it is important that these mistakes be avoided or minimized. Conceptual work on specifying the appropriate model or models for measuring these interrelationships should therefore begin immediately so that the required data can be specified and the data collection process begun. It is important to emphasize that while this conceptual work will not produce immediate payoffs, any delays in beginning it will only delay the availability of useful results.

The technique which we have used in estimating transportation demand functions is regression analysis of observations drawn from the urban environment. It is possible to perform experiments to generate observations for analysis by conducting demonstration projects, rather than relying on the observations given by the existing environment. There is no compelling reason to restrict the research to either approach, and indeed both should be encouraged. However, there is one disadvantage in using the results of a demonstration project as a basis for analyzing demand. The demonstration will of necessity be a temporary change in price or service and therefore will not invoke the same response as a permanent change, *e.g.*, people will not change their places of work or residence to adapt to the change. For this reason careful attention should be given to the design of any contemplated demonstration projects so that useful results can be elicited. The Department of Housing and Urban Development demonstration projects, for example, produced almost no knowledge of the effects of service improvements on ridership response since the demonstrations were essentially regarded as a one-time subsidy. No provision was made to design experiments that would meaningfully test stated hypotheses, no provision was made for data collection, and accordingly it is impossible to obtain useful analytical results from the projects.[a]

From the standpoint of system cost and performance, the most pressing research needs concern the cost and performance parameters of new developments such as dual-mode vehicles and ramp metering.

There is also a need for a careful analysis of the full social costs of urban highways. As mentioned earlier, the existing studies have concluded that operating and capital costs are covered by user charges. But little is known about the external costs — aesthetics, social dislocation, etc. — and such costs as law enforcement and traffic safety are not usually counted. Many of these externalities are very difficult or impossible to quantify, of course, It is frequently possible, however, to turn the measurement problem around so that reasonable judgments can be made. That is, an estimate could be made of the excess of user charges over capital and operating costs. Then the external costs could be itemized. Using value and policy judgments, the excess user charges could be compared to the list of externalities to see if a reasonable balance exists. This research is needed to appraise existing user charges and to guide the allocation of investment between highway and transit.

[a]This point is discussed by Martin Wohl, *Users of Urban Transportation Services and Their Income Circumstances* (unpublished), The Rand Corporation, June 1968.

9 Conclusions

This study has examined and evaluated a program of free transit service for metropolitan area users. This concluding chapter first summarizes the results of our analysis of the demand for urban passenger travel. This is followed by estimates of the costs of providing free transit service. We then discuss the different objectives which a program of free transit service seeks to achieve, and review the comparative effectiveness of free transit versus alternative means of promoting these same objectives. Following this is a discussion of the administrative and income redistributional considerations of a free transit program. Finally, we summarize the major needs for additional research to evaluate programs for urban mass transportation service.

Demand for Urban Passenger Transportation

We developed an econometric model of urban passenger travel demands based on Boston data. The model measures the relationship between the number of trips by purpose and mode (transit and auto) and the variables which give rise to travel demand. These variables are the socioeconomic and land-use characteristics of the origin and destination zones together with the interzonal times and costs of travel by each of the alternative modes.

The model indicates first that transit demand is very inelastic with respect to changes in fares.[a] For shopping trips, the fare elasticity (taken at the means of the variables) is only about -.32, while for work trips it is about -.17. These low elasticities indicate that sizeable fare reductions cannot be counted on to stimulate transit usage greatly. Indeed, they suggest that an increase in fares would substantially increase transit revenues.

The second general conclusion to be drawn from the demand model is that most of the cross-elasticities are very low or negligible. The cross-elasticities measure the effect of a change in the travel time or cost of one mode on the demand for the other mode. The low cross-elasticities indicate that it will be very difficult to divert auto travelers to transit by lowering fares or by improving service, although, the results do indicate that work trips are more likely to be diverted to transit than shopping trips, and reductions in transit travel times (especially non-line-haul times) will be more consequential in this regard than reductions in fares. For work trips the non-line-haul time cross-elasticity of .373 is about 2.5 times the fare cross-elasticity of .138.

Third, travel demand is more responsive to reductions in travel time than to reductions in fares. For shopping trips transit demand is about twice as

---

[a]Elasticity can be defined as the percentage change in demand resulting from a 1 percent change in one of the explanatory variables, everything else remaining constant.

responsive to changes in travel time as it is to changes in fares (*i.e.*, the elasticity is -.593 compared to -.323). For work trips, the elasticity with respect to transit non-line-haul time is about 3.5 times the fare elasticity (-.709 compared to -.17) while the line-haul time elasticity is about double the fare elasticity (-.39 to -.17).

Finally, there is some evidence that transit ridership is more responsive to improvements in collection and distribution service than to increases in line-haul speeds. If this conclusion is accurate, it indicates that proposals for rapid transit or express bus service, which chiefly reduce line-haul time, may be less attractive to users than improvements in the collection and distribution service such as increasing the geographical coverage of the system (*e.g.*, increasing the number of cross-town lines) and increasing the schedule frequency.

Cost of Free Transit Service

We have made estimates of both the nationwide costs of providing free transit service and the costs for the Boston metropolitan area, the case study which we examined. In both cases, the cost of the subsidy is the full operating and capital costs of the existing system plus the cost of accommodating the increased ridership induced by the free fare, minus the expenses of fare collection. We estimate that the nationwide costs of providing free transit service are on the order of $2 billion per year, assuming that roughly the level of service which now prevails is maintained. Approximately $1.75 billion of this amount is the cost of providing the current service; the balance is the cost of the additional capacity needed to accommodate the increased ridership. The annual figure of $2 billion can probably be regarded as a lower limit since over time the costs would tend to grow in order to provide service for a growing population. There is also likely to be a tendency for communities to want to improve the level of transit service if it can be done without the community directly incurring the costs of the improvement, which, of course, would also increase the annual cost of the subsidy.

For the Boston area, the annual costs are on the order of $75 million. Since the population in the areas served by the MBTA is about 2.6 million people, this is about $30 per person per year. As with the nationwide subsidy, this figure includes capital and operating costs and takes into account the capacity expansion needed to accommodate the additional riders induced by the free fare. We estimate that the elimination of fares in the Boston area would increase ridership by about 32 percent.[b] The annualized cost of capacity expansion is estimated to be about $8.4 million, about 12 percent of the current MBTA costs of about $70.4 million. The figure of $75 million also incorporates a deduction of $3.5 million per year, representing the savings from eliminating fare collection, which include the costs of collecting fares, maintaining fare collection equipment, and the costs of the revenue accounting function. In Boston, these savings amount to slightly less than 5 percent of transit system costs.

A corresponding deduction was not made from the estimated nationwide subsidy because these savings are very speculative for the nation as a whole and are likely to be very small. This is because the major portion of the savings (about $2 million of the $3.5 million in Boston) is the labor cost of fare collection agents in subway stations, but this component would not be saved by transit systems which do not have rapid transit service. Moreover, because these collection agents also provide information and protection functions which would be needed even if fare collection were eliminated, not all systems which have rapid transit would be able to eliminate these costs fully.

**Relative Efficiency of Free Transit
in Meeting Objectives**

To evaluate free transit service, it is necessary to compare its effectiveness in achieving given objectives with the efficiency of meeting these objectives by other means. The principal method of evaluation, therefore, was to compare free transit with improvements in the quality of transit service, on a cost-effectiveness basis. As mentioned above, improvements in service are found to be a more efficient means of meeting objectives than reductions in fares. The goals commonly presented in arguments for free transit service include the following:

1) To improve the accessibility of job opportunities for ghetto residents.
2) To aid in revitalizing the downtowns.
3) To divert auto travelers to transit, thereby reducing mounting rush-hour highway congestion, decreasing air pollution, and reducing the demand for parking facilities.

Each of these objectives is discussed in turn.

Improve Accessibility of Jobs to Ghetto Residents

A comprehensive free transit program appears to be a costly and largely ineffective means of providing ghetto residents access to job centers. The basic problem is that the transit system often provides reasonable service only for the radial trip pattern that was predominant several decades ago rather than for the cross-city trips which are now needed to move ghetto residents to dispersed job

[b]About a 28 percent increase is directly attributable to the elimination of fares. A 4 percent increase arises form the reduction of headways (hence, waiting times) resulting from the added capacity required to accommodate the increased riders.

opportunities. Good transit service is usually available from the ghetto to the downtown, but the service to the scattered job areas is often indirect, infrequent, and extremely time-consuming. Making the existing service free will not correct this problem.

A more effective and far less costly approach is to provide improved transit service from the ghettos to job centers. This service could be made free to ghetto residents for far less than the subsidy needed to finance a comprehensive free transit program. In the Boston case study, we located the low-income residential areas and the low-skilled job centers and estimated the cost of providing very good bus service between the residential areas and the job centers. The estimated cost of these service improvements was approximately $4.3 million per year (for both operating costs and capital recovery). This is only about 6 percent of the estimated annual cost for a comprehensive program of free transit service for the Boston area.

Revitalize the Downtown

There has been a profound change in the relative importance of central cities in the postwar period. Retail sales, employment, and population of the central cities have either declined or remained roughly constant while enormous growth has occurred in the metropolitan areas outside the central cities. The relative importance of the factors which have led to urban decentralization is not at all well understood, but most sources agree that fundamental economic and technological changes underlie the trend toward decentralization. In the face of these basic forces, it may be very difficult and costly to preserve the downtown in its traditional role and it may even be impossible to do so.

Nevertheless, it is reasonable to examine the relative effectiveness of a program of free transit service as a means of stimulating downtown activity. The demand model indicates that free transit would increase downtown shopping trips by about one-third. The zero cross-elasticity in the demand model suggests that the fare reduction would not decrease automobile shopping trips. This suggests that rather than diverting trips from suburban shopping centers to the downtown, the free fare would simply increase transit trips to the downtown.

This could represent less carefully planned shopping trips, as a result of a reduction in the money cost of an additional trip, by people who are already using the transit system, or it could represent trips made by shoppers who previously walked. It is questionable whether the increase in trips would result in a sizeable increase in downtown sales if there were no diversion from suburban shopping centers.

From a cost-effectiveness viewpoint, it may be more efficient to subsidize service improvements rather than fares. We calculated the cost of adding service (*i.e.*, improving the collection and distribution system to reduce non-line-haul travel time) where service improvements could be measured relatively easily and found that transit shopping trips to downtown Boston could be increased on the order of 15 percent for about $12 million per year. Therefore, about half of the stimulus of the free-fare subsidy to Boston shopping could be achieved for less than one-sixth of the cost by allocating the subsidy funds to service improvements.

Reduce Highway Congestion, Air Pollution, and Parking
Problems by Diverting Travelers from the Automobile

The effectiveness of a program of free transit in reducing auto congestion depends on the cross-elasticity of auto demand with respect to transit fares. Our results indicate that free transit would reduce auto work trips by about 14 percent, but would divert few shopping trips to the transit system from the auto. Adjusting this figure for the ratio of work to total auto trips yields a reduction in rush-hour auto traffic of 6 to 9 percent.

Again, a more efficient means of reducing rush-hour auto traffic appears to be to improve transit service. Our calculations show that improvements in the collection and distribution system, costing about one-sixth the public funds required by free transit, would reduce auto rush-hour traffic by 4 to 6 percent, compared to 6 to 9 percent for free transit.

The automobile is a major contributor to air pollution problems in our large urban centers. However, because free transit is not likely to result in substantial diversion of auto traffic, it is unlikely to produce a major reduction in auto emissions. We estimate that the diversion in auto traffic induced by free transit would reduce vehicle emissions by about 4.5 percent and 3 percent in the morning and evening rush respectively. It is unlikely that such a reduction will have much effect on ambient air quality. By contrast, the control devices for 1968 and later model cars, when properly maintained, will reduce emissions of hydrocarbons and of carbon monoxide by about two-thirds as compared with earlier model cars without exhaust controls.

The reduction in auto travel resulting from the diversion of auto trips to transit will reduce parking requirements, particularly in the downtown areas. Since the principal diversion resulting from free transit will be auto work trips, the significance of the effect is increased. The desirable number of parking spaces for each Control Business District (CBD) work trip by auto is estimated to be .500 and for each CBD nonwork trip is .147. Because of the differences in parking turnover between work and nonwork auto trips, the reduction of one work trip may provide parking space for at least 3.4 nonwork trips. The increase in parking spaces available for nonwork tripmakers is likely to have additional stimulating effects because shopping trips are highly responsive to the cost and convenience of parking. However, as discussed earlier, a more efficient means of diverting auto work trips appears to be the improvement of transit service.

Administrative and Income Redistributional Considerations

A free transit subsidy program will present difficult administrative problems. These stem primarily from the lack of market information that is usually obtained from prices. With free transit, as in any public investment program based on other than "market" benefits or other obvious indices of the worth of expenditures, a means must be devised by which the net benefits of public investment are measured and evaluated so that a rational allocation of resources can be obtained. This involves both specifying criteria for making spending decisions within a given operating budget and providing guidelines for expansion or curtailment of services as cities grow or transportation needs change. There is also a risk that public subsidies will reduce the incentive to operate efficiently.

One of the most significant aspects of a subsidized transit system is the method of raising the revenue to finance the operation. Although free transit may be free to the users, it certainly cannot be regarded as free to society. Regardless of how these resources are paid for, the method of financing may create transfers of income from one group in society to another.

There are three general types of income transfers to be considered: redistributions of income between users and nonusers, redistributions among regions, and redistributions from one socioeconomic class to another. These transfers are very difficult to quantify and we make no attempt to do so, but it is possible to identify some of them.

To the extent that free transit would be funded from any form of general or broad-based taxation there will be an income transfer from nonusers to users. This form of financing would also transfer income from rural ro urban regions. Within the urban area, income would be transferred from suburban to central city merchants and residents if the tax incidence did not compensate for the differences in service. Redistribution between socioeconomic groups (and between regions) is now in effect where long-haul, low density routes to wealthy suburbs are underpriced and receive a cross-subsidy from short-haul, high density routes in the core city. Where this transfer of funds is not compensated by tax differences, income is redistributed from poor to rich. To the extent that federal taxes are more progressive than state or municipal taxes, federally supported free transit service may result in more desirable transfers between socioeconomic groups than now occurs in some communities.

Research Needs

The need for a better understanding of the demand for urban transportation overshadows all other research needs. This study benefited greatly from a model of urban transportation demand developed in a previous study, but this model is still very primitive and has numerous limitations. The model aggregates over all forms of public transit which makes it impossible to investigate separately the demand for different types of transit and probably substantially reduces the accuracy of the estimated transit parameters. Virtually nothing is known about the cross-elasticity between peak and off-peak travel times.

The models that have been developed on demand are short run; they assume that land-use patterns are given. A basic need is to model the interrelationship between land-use and the transportation system. Modeling the time period required for the adjustments in land use caused by changes in the transportation system, will require the gathering of extensive and costly time-series data, which are not now available. One mistake that has been made in collecting urban transportation data in the past is that questionnaires have been prepared and the data collected before the model for which the data were to be used was designed. As a result, essential data were overlooked and much of the available data could only be used with difficulty. Extensive and efficient data collection cannot take place in a vacuum. Because of the basic cost and long lead times involved in developing the data base for investigating the interrelationship between the transportation system and urban development, it is important that these mistakes be avoided or minimized.

About the Authors

Thomas A. Domencich is Vice President and **Gerald Kraft** is President of Charles River Associates Incorporated.